S0-FFX-962

Contents

1 9 9 8

PERSONAL PRAYER

journal

Devote Yourselves
to Prayer, Being
Watchful & Thankful

WORLD WIDE PUBLICATIONS
Minneapolis, Minnesota 55403

1998 Personal Prayer Journal Deluxe

© 1997 World Wide Publications

In compliance with copyright restrictions, no portion of these materials may be reproduced in any form without written permission of the publisher: World Wide Publications, 1303 Hennepin Avenue, Minneapolis, Minnesota 55403.

World Wide Publications is the publishing ministry of the Billy Graham Evangelistic Association.

All Scripture quotations, unless otherwise noted, are taken from The Holy Bible, New International Version, 1973, 1978, 1984 International Bible Society. Used by permission of Zondervan Bible Publishers.

ISBN: 0-89066-287-8

Printed in Canada

The Importance of Prayer

*P*rayer is our most important work as Christians. It is a journey filled with the satisfaction of helping the helpless, and of seeing the purposes of God fulfilled and the strategies of Satan thwarted. In the unseen arena of prayer the real work of God is forged. We often see the results in the visible world, but God is moving behind the scenes, acting in response to those who labor daily in prayer.

Exodus 17 illustrates this principle vividly. As the Israelite army fought the Amalekites on the plain of Rephidim, Moses stood on a hill overlooking the battle. Whenever he held up the staff of God, Israel prevailed. But when he lowered the staff, the Amalekites gained the advantage. A clear principle of prayer emerges from this account: God acts in response to the prayers of his intercessors, supernaturally enabling those he has called to accomplish the assigned task. Moses' part in the victory, though probably unseen and unnoticed by those in the fight, was vital.

Our role in the work of God throughout the world may be unnoticed, unseen, unappreciated. But, like Moses, God calls us to "hold up the staff of God"—to pray. In fact, God is looking "for a man among them who would build up the wall and stand before me in the gap on behalf of the land so I would not have to destroy it, but I found none" (Ezekiel 22:30). We need to take our part in the plan and program of God seriously, developing the attitude that Samuel had toward Israel when he said, "As for me, far be it from me that I should sin against the Lord by failing to pray for you" (1 Samuel 12:23).

Prayer is work. Prayer is hard work. But prayer is a holy work as well—

vital and indispensable. God has a more difficult time finding people for *prayer* than he does for any other assignment.

The Personal Prayer Journal Is Designed

. . . .

1. To provide practical insights from God's Word on prayer.

2. To provide a suggested plan for a prayer ministry that is manageable, measurable, and useful.

3. To provide the means of making prayer ministry a reality.

> In order to make a tool like the *Personal Prayer Journal* work, we need the determination to be faithful to the commitment.

1. Our primary responsibility is to be faithful to pray. The results of our prayers are God's responsibility.

2. We need to be realistic in our prayer ministry. Faithfulness to a short, daily prayer time is more desirable than occasional faithfulness to an unrealistic larger time commitment.

3. We should make daily entries of significant prayer items in the space provided on the calendar pages. These will become a source of tremendous encouragement and motivation as we look back at the written record of how God answered specific prayers.

4. The Personal Prayer Journal is designed for only one aspect of our spiritual life—prayer. We must not neglect regular reading and meditation in God's Word.

Principles of Prayer

As we begin to develop a personal prayer strategy, we need to examine some principles of prayer from God's Word. Three vital aspects of prayer are:

🌱 Attitudes in prayer 🌱 Obstacles to prayer 🌱 Answers to prayer

Attitudes in Prayer

Prayer is conversation with God. But when we talk with God it is not just like any other conversation. There are several qualities that should mark our attitudes as we converse with our Creator:

Awe. When John the apostle saw the glorified Christ, he "fell at his feet as though dead" (Revelation 1:17). When the prophet Isaiah had his vision of the throne room of God, he exclaimed, "Woe to me! . . . I am ruined! For I am a man of unclean lips, and I live among a people of unclean lips, and my eyes have seen the King, the Lord Almighty" (Isaiah 6:5).

Yet, as A. W. Tozer has said,

We go to God as we send a boy to a grocery store with a long written list, "God, give me this," and our gracious God often gives us what we want. But I think God is disappointed because we make him no more than a source of what we want.

Awe simply means being constantly amazed at who God is and that he would even allow us to address him as "Father."

Helplessness. We must be genuinely convinced of our own inability to accomplish the thing for which we are praying to God. O. Hallesby, in his classic book, *Prayer,* highlights this truth when he says:

> Be not anxious because of your helplessness. Above all, do not let it prevent you
> from praying. Helplessness is the real secret and the impelling power of prayer.
> You should therefore rather try to thank God for the feeling of helplessness which
> He has given you. It is one of the greatest gifts which God can impart to us. For *it
> is only when we are helpless* that we open our hearts to Jesus and let Him help us
> in our distress, according to His grace and mercy.

The apostle Paul similarly speaks of our total inability to accomplish
anything on our own in the spiritual realm. He confesses, "You see, at just
the right time, when we were still powerless, Christ died for the ungodly"
(Romans 5:6). And again in Romans 8:26 he says, "The Spirit helps us in
our weakness. We do not know what we ought to pray for."

The proper starting place in prayer, then, is an awe of God, which in
turn makes us see our own helplessness. It is the realization that we are
totally powerless within ourselves to make our prayers happen. Our helplessness induces prayer.

Faith. But it takes more than helplessness. It is faith that shapes the
cries of our hearts into genuine prayer. Hallesby points out that,

> Without faith there can be no prayer, no matter how great our helplessness may
> be. Helplessness united with faith produces prayer. Without faith our helpless-
> ness would only be a vain cry of distress in the night.

The writer of Hebrews agrees:

> And without faith it is impossible to please God, because anyone who comes to
> him must believe that he exists and that he rewards those who earnestly seek him
> (11:6).

But faith is often the very thing we feel that we lack in our prayer life.
Perhaps we do not understand that in the very act of praying we are
demonstrating faith. By going to God, we exercise genuine faith. It may be
a young faith, but it *is* faith! We have "faith enough" when we turn to
Jesus in our helplessness. The *results* of prayer are the concern of God.
Our concern is to come to him in prayer with the awareness that we are
helpless in ourselves.

Confidence. The essence of faith is our confidence in God's ability to do what he has promised. Abraham stands as our clearest illustration of confident faith:

> Yet he did not waver through unbelief regarding the promise of God, but was strengthened in his faith and gave glory to God, being fully persuaded that God had power to do what he had promised (Romans 4:20–21).

Too often we unconsciously shift our faith from confidence in God's ability to do what he has promised, to confidence in our ability to believe he will do a certain thing. In other words, we put our confidence in our faith rather than in God! Jesus makes it clear that the *size* of our faith is not what matters when he says, "I tell you the truth, if you have faith as small as a mustard seed, you can say to this mountain, 'Move from here to there' and it will move. Nothing will be impossible for you" (Matthew 17:20). It is the *object* of our faith—God—that is the basis of our confidence in prayer.

Persistence. In Matthew 7:7 Jesus says, "Ask and it will be given to you; seek and you will find; knock and the door will be opened to you." This verse translated literally says, "Ask and keep on asking . . . seek and keep on seeking . . . knock and keep on knocking." It shows us the importance of persistent prayer, of continuing to bring our prayers to God. Even Jesus, on the night of his betrayal, brought his anguished plea to the Father three times before relenting.

Obstacles to Prayer

Even the most mature Christians will sometimes feel that their prayers are not getting "beyond the ceiling." There are several things that can seriously hinder our prayer life:

Unconfessed sin. David confessed, "If I had cherished sin in my heart, the Lord would not have listened" (Psalm 66:18). Isaiah tells us, "Surely the arm of the Lord is not too short to save, nor his ear too dull to hear. But your iniquities have separated you from your God; your sins have hidden his face from you, so that he will not hear" (Isaiah 59:1–2).

Sin renders our prayers useless because it alienates us from the object of our prayers—God. When we are out of fellowship with God due to unconfessed sin in our lives, our prayers are powerless monologues. We need to confess our sins of anger, lust, envy, gossip, or whatever else that has become a barrier between us and our Father. The basis of our access in prayer is fellowship with God.

Broken fellowship with others. Too often, "fellowship" is mistakenly understood to be an activity, when in fact it is a condition. Fellowship is not so much something we do as something we are either in or out of. The apostle John illuminates this for us:

> If we claim to have fellowship with him yet walk in the darkness, we lie and do not live by the truth. But if we walk in the light, as he is in the light, we have fellowship with one another, and the blood of Jesus, his Son, purifies us from all sin (1 John 1:6–7).

It is clear from this passage that our relationship with God is inseparably linked to our relationship with other believers. We cannot go to God in prayer when we are out of fellowship with one of his other children. Jesus emphasized this truth to his disciples in the Sermon on the Mount when he said:

> Therefore, if you are offering your gift at the altar and there remember that your brother has something against you, leave your gift there in front of the altar. First go and be reconciled to your brother; then come and offer your gift (Matthew 5:23–24).

Restitution of broken relationships is a prerequisite to effective prayer. This principle applies to relationships both inside and outside the church; it is especially relevant within the home. The apostle Peter said that conflict between spouses will "hinder" their prayers (1 Peter 3:7).

We can safely say in the light of these Scriptures that if we are not on speaking terms with God's people, we are not on speaking terms with God either. As with unconfessed sin in general, we should make immediate efforts to restore any broken relationship before we resume the ministry of intercession. If restoration is not possible immediately, we need to confess this broken fellowship to God and make a commitment to *him* to deal with it as soon as possible.

Wrong motives. A final obstacle to prayer has to do with the intention of our hearts. James warns us,

> When you ask, you do not receive, because you ask with wrong motives, that you may spend what you get on your pleasures (James 4:3).

If we pray for things that will feed that part of us known as our "sinful nature" (Romans 7:18), we cannot expect those prayers to reach the heart of God. Why not? Because God's goal for each one of us is to transform us into the likeness of his Son, Jesus Christ (Romans 8:29). God is not pleased to hear prayer that is contrary to his plans and purposes for our lives. But John assures us that we will be heard when we pray according to his will (1 John 5:14—15).

Our motives, the driving force behind our requests, are crucial factors that can limit the effectiveness of prayer.

Answers to Prayer

God has promised to answer our prayers. Yet we need to understand the various forms an answer to prayer can assume. God's answers may sometimes be either a simple "yes" or "no." At other times, the answer may be more complex. The following are four possible ways that God may answer our prayers:

Request granted. God's Word contains a multitude of promises that we will receive what we ask God for. This is especially true if we pray according to God's specific will for our lives—those things that he wants for us (1 John 5:14—15). Sometimes we pray specifically and God answers specifically. This is a marvelous experience, one that easily fosters courage and motivation for further prayer.

Request granted, but not yet. Isaiah 55:8—9 instructs us that God's thoughts and methods are "higher" than ours—"as the heavens are higher than the earth." Sometimes God's timetable is different from ours! God's answer to our prayers in this case is indeed yes, but we must yield to his schedule. This is an answer, and it is an affirmative answer, but we can easily miss seeing the answer, or believe that God hasn't heard us, simply because the answer hasn't arrived on time. Patience and persistence in prayer are sometimes needed to ensure that we keep looking for God's answer.

Request granted, but look elsewhere. At Jesus' final meal with his disciples, the night of his betrayal, he began to wash their feet (John 13:1—10). Peter was quite offended and when he tried to stop our Lord, Jesus told him that his perspective was wrong (vv. 6—7). Peter was looking so hard for what he expected to see (a conquering Messiah), that he failed to see what was there (a servant Messiah). There are times in prayer when we make a request, fully convinced of what form the answer will take. If God then answers in an unexpected fashion, we may fail to see the answer. We, like Peter, have our minds so made up about what should happen, we fail to see what is actually happening. We need to guard ourselves from unconsciously dictating how God will answer. We must give him the liberty to be God!

Request denied. In our relationship with God, sometimes a gradual but serious shift occurs in our own minds regarding who serves whom. Christians can easily forget that God is not a magic genie who jumps at every command. God is God. He is always at liberty to say no to our requests—not capriciously or maliciously, of course, for that would be a denial of his character. But he is still Lord of all. Times will come in our lives when God will deliberately withhold granting requests because of their ultimate effect on our lives or the lives of others. Perhaps the development of certain character qualities in our lives is more vital than the request sought. Withholding answers to prayer must always be understood as his ultimate *protection*, never as *punishment*. Our responsibility during these times of painful denial is to trust in what we know of God's love for us.

The Practice of Prayer

Without this final section, all that has been previously said is merely lifeless information. Talking about prayer is not prayer. To pray effectively, we need to know when, with whom, how, and what to pray.

When to Pray

David prayed faithfully in the morning, evening, and often at noon (Psalm 5:3 and 55:17). Our Lord also spent times in prayer during early morning hours and late at night (Mark 1:35 and 6:46 ff.). Much can be said for "opening and closing" each day in communion with God. Often these times provide the most privacy and greatest freedom to be reflective and quiet.

Abraham's chief servant, sent by his master to secure a bride for Isaac, communed with God in the midst of a busy schedule, surrounded by strangers (Genesis 24:11—14). He prayed quietly in his heart (v. 45) in the midst of his work. It is acceptable and advisable to pray throughout the day as well as in the morning and evening. We need not be in the privacy of our homes to seek the face of God. Often, the Lord will bring to mind a person or an issue at the "oddest time." We need to seize these moments and use them to offer short, specific prayers back to God. Learning to respond to the unexpected promptings of the Holy Spirit is vital to a vibrant prayer life.

It is good to have a set time of daily prayer, but it is also important to seize the "eternal moments" that God gives throughout each day.

With Whom to Pray

Jesus exhorts us to shun praying in public in order to impress others, and encourages us to pray "in secret" (Matthew 6:5—6). Private prayer will undoubtedly occupy the largest portion of our total prayer life. During these moments of solitude we can unveil our hearts before him who sees us as we are and yet loves us with an everlasting love. During these private hours we can intercede for the world that exists outside our private place. Here we can plead, weep, or rejoice over issues that matter little to anyone but us and God. Private prayer should be a priority.

But Jesus also speaks of praying with "two or three" (Matthew 18:19—20). The early Christians prayed together often (Acts 4:23—24; 12:12). A sweetness of fellowship and a sense of strength come when God's people go to him together in prayer.

God's Word holds before us models of private and corporate prayer; both are vital and should have a place in our prayer life.

How to Pray

It is more important *that* we pray than *how* we pray. Those who pray best are those who pray most. Yet, for some, a very broad format is helpful—a sort of "skeleton" model onto which personal detail can be added.

A model for how to pray is captured in the acrostic: ACTS. Each letter stands for a specific aspect of prayer, arranged in a very natural order:

A— Adoration (worship)

C— Confession (of specific sins)

T— Thanksgiving (gratitude)

S— Supplication (specific requests)

Adoration. Worship begins and ends with who God is. Beginning our prayer time with adoration immediately places us in the position of a creature in the presence of its Creator. Adoration is simply acknowledging to God what he has revealed about himself. One helpful way to cultivate an attitude of adoration is to take actual phrases from Scripture and "pray them back" to God, using them as springboards of thought on who God is and what he is like. Some of the many appropriate passages for this purpose are Job 38; 1 Chronicles 29:10—13; Psalm 19:1—2; Psalm 84; Psalm 95:1—7; and many other Psalms.

Not only is this the proper starting place for prayer, it is a crucial driving force in our entire Christian life. As we worship, we must be sure that the One we worship is indeed the living God.

Confession. The closer we draw to God himself, the more we sense our own sinfulness. Again like Isaiah, a glimpse of God's glory will cause us to exclaim, "Woe to me" (Isaiah 6:5), as we realize how far we fall short of his glory.

The natural consequence of genuine adoration is sincere confession. It is reasonable that as we worship God, the awareness of our personal sin becomes greater.

Confession is the second step in prayer: agreeing with God that specific conduct and attitudes in our lives are wrong. We should name the sin and ask God to forgive us. During this period of confession, we may also ask God to make us aware of other sins in our life that we are unaware of or have neglected to deal with.

Thanksgiving. Our immediate response after confession is thanksgiving. David said, "Blessed is he whose transgressions are forgiven" (Psalm 32:1). We can certainly thank God for forgiving us of the sins we have just confessed. But gratitude to God should encompass more than forgiveness. Paul told the Colossians,

> And whatever you do, whether in word or deed, do it all in the name of the Lord Jesus, giving thanks to God the Father through him (Colossians 3:17).

Thanksgiving causes us to acknowledge God's existence, his love, and his care. It reminds us of his goodness. In short, thanksgiving forces us to keep God in our thoughts.

We should thank God for all the blessings we can see in our lives— health, friends, guidance, and answered prayer. But we should also verbally thank him for all that is ours that we can't see, such as, our adoption as his children, our inheritance in heaven, the ministry of angels in our lives, the new body that will be ours for eternity, and the permanent gift of the Holy Spirit.

By giving thanks, which is simply expressing gratitude for what we have, we prevent our focus from shifting to what we *don't* have. Satan loves to distract God's children from thanksgiving, because he can accomplish much in a heart that is ungrateful. Thanksgiving is a powerful weapon against Satan's tactics.

Supplication. The last step in the ACTS model is supplication— bringing our requests to God. If we are faithful in the first three steps, this last step will not degenerate into a spiritual "shopping list." Too often, when we think of prayer, our minds rush immediately to supplication because we have not cultivated the practice of adoration, confession, and thanksgiving. Supplication by itself can become selfish, but when it follows our adoration, confession, and thanksgiving, it balances our prayer life.

What to Pray

Nine times in John's Gospel Jesus commands us to "ask" in prayer. Supplication is God's idea, not just a result of our need. The Lord wants us to ask certain things of him. But what should we pray for? In the Scriptures, God indicates what *he* wishes us to pray for:

Self. Pray for personal growth in Christlikeness and a sensitivity to God (Colossians 1:9–10).

Family. Pray for spouse, children, and children's children; pray for an unbroken heritage of love for God (Proverbs 20:7; Isaiah 54:13).

Community. Pray that God will show us our part in the area where we live (Jeremiah 29:7). Pray for a visible witness of unity among God's people in our communities (Philippians 4:2–3).

Church. Pray for a sense of unity in vision and heart. Pray for a desire to please God rather than each other (Philippians 2:1–4).

Church leadership. Pray for a deep sensitivity to the will of God, clarity of vision, and a desire for personal holiness (Hebrews 13:17; 1 Timothy 5:17). Pray for a deep conviction for one-on-one disciple making (2 Timothy 2:2).

The nation. Pray for national repentance and a consciousness of who God is (Psalm 33:12; Proverbs 14:34).

Leaders in government. Pray for wisdom and integrity, and an awareness of their accountability to God (1 Timothy 2:1—2; Romans 13:1).

Nonbelievers. Pray for understanding of salvation, and an openness to the Spirit's promptings. Pray that Christians will be sensitive to the nonbelievers in their lives (1 Timothy 2:1—6).

The sick. Pray for God's healing or assurance (James 5:14—16).

Those in prison. Pray for an understanding of Christ's forgiveness. Pray for strength to resist sin, and encouragement against loneliness (Hebrews 13:3; Colossians 4:18).

Children. Pray for the unborn children who face abortion. Pray for those whose lives are shattered by divorce (Malachi 4:6; Matthew 19:14).

A Weekly Prayer Strategy

Monday — *Family*

🌿 Pray for immediate family members (you may want to get actual requests from them individually).
🌿 Pray for friends of family members.

Tuesday — *Church*

🌿 Pray for the leadership in your local fellowship.
🌿 Pray for the marriages and families of your church leadership; they are key targets of Satan.
🌿 Pray for specific ministries within your church.

Wednesday — *Community*

🌿 Pray for community leaders.
🌿 Pray for the churches in your community.
🌿 Pray for Christian endeavors in your community (e.g., evangelism outreaches, pro-life efforts, ministries to the homeless, etc.).

Thursday — *Nation*

🌿 Pray for our president.
🌿 Pray for elected officials from your state.
🌿 Pray for the seminaries that are training our future pastors and Christian leaders.

Friday — *World*

🌿 Pray for world peace.
🌿 Pray for the missionaries your church supports.
🌿 Pray for nations that are "closed" to the gospel. (Refer regularly to the "Prayer Concerns Around the World" section at the end of this Journal.)

Saturday — *Afflicted*

🌿 Pray for those ministering in difficult circumstances in developing countries.
🌿 Pray for those in prison.
🌿 Pray for those from your church who are hospitalized or sick.
🌿 Pray for the children affected by divorce.

Ideas

• • •

Akey element in keeping prayer personal is making it creative. Often, routine is the assassin of effective prayer. Below are some ideas for creative prayer.

🍃 Make a "prayer book" of pictures. This would work well for family, leaders, and missionaries. Often *seeing* people gives us a personal burden as we pray for them.

🍃 When praying for the nation and the world, pray about the front-page events of your local newspaper.

🍃 Make a list of needy people in your church or neighborhood. Pray for them with your family and explore ways that various family members can reach out to them.

🍃 Make a list of all the leaders in your church and their specific areas of ministry. Ask them for specific requests from time to time.

🍃 As you use this Journal and read the suggested Scriptures, keep notes of the needs and people who come to mind and pray for them. Then, think of ways you could help answer each prayer need. For instance, who among your acquaintances needs a "cup of cold water" (Matthew 10:42) from you today?

🍃 Have your family find out more about some of the countries listed in the "Prayer Concerns" section (page 129). Using sources such as *National Geographic,* do a pictorial display in a scrap book or on a bulletin board and use that as a focal point for prayer.

🍃 Get a list of all missionaries and organizations your church supports. Many have monthly newsletters that keep you informed so you can pray more specifically. Perhaps pray for one or two missionaries or organizations each month.

Caught in the Act of Prayer!

A young president of an East Coast company instructed his secretary not to disturb him because he had an important appointment. The chairman of the board arrived and said, "I want to see Mr. Jones."

The secretary answered, "I'm sorry. He cannot be disturbed. He has a special appointment."

The chairman became angry and banged open the door. He saw the president of the corporation in prayer. The chairman softly closed the door and asked the secretary, "Is that usual?"

She answered, "Yes, sir, every morning."

The chairman replied, "No wonder we come to him for advice."

— BILLY GRAHAM*

*From *Decision* magazine, October 1988, page 3. Used by permission.

Prayer Concerns:

Answers:

27 ✿ Monday

* HAVING A PROBLEM WITH
  FORGIVENESS

* SHOULD I CHANGE JOBS?

* INCREASING VIOLENCE IN
  SOCIETY

Luke 19:1—29

* LEARNING MORE
  ABOUT LOVE

* WHERE CAN I BEST
  SERVE CHRIST?

* SAW HOW GENTLE
  WORDS CAN HELP

The following pages consist of journal sections for every day of the year. There is a place provided to record your prayer concerns for each day; remember the recommendation that a short, daily prayer time may be better than occasional, longer commitments. There's also a place to record the answers you receive to your prayers. Try to remember what you prayed for from day to day, and be aware of the different ways God may be answering those prayers.

Notice also the suggested daily Scripture readings, which will take you through the entire New Testament in a year. Prayer is conversation with God, and as you read these passages you can think of them as "conversation openers" between you and God. Let him speak to you through his Word; then spend some time with him in prayer. Maybe you'll even find answers to prayer in the suggested daily reading.

Finally, remember the "Prayer Concerns Around the World," listed in the final section of your *Personal Prayer Journal.* The many needs represented can seem overwhelming, yet we must be faithful in prayer, and trust God to meet the needs as he sees fit.

May God bless you as you faithfully seek him in the fellowship of prayer.

Paper White Narcissus

Cast all your anxiety on him
because he cares for you.
—1 Peter 5:7

The way to worry about nothing is to pray about
everything.   —Anonymous

JANUARY 1998
S M T W T F S
            1 2 3
4 5 6 7 8 9 10
11 12 13 14 15 16 17
18 19 20 21 22 23 24
25 26 27 28 29 30 31

Prayer Concerns:

Answers:

December 28 ❧ *Sunday*

29 ❧ *Monday*

30 ❧ *Tuesday*

31 ❧ *Wednesday*

1 ❧ *Thursday*

Matthew 1

2 ❧ *Friday*

Matthew 2

3 ❧ *Saturday*

Matthew 3

Paper White Narcissus

Delight yourself in the Lord
and he will give you the desires
of your heart. —Psalm 37:4

Happiness consists in the attainment of our desires, and
in our having only right desires. —Augustine

JANUARY 1998

S	M	T	W	T	F	S
				1	2	3
4	5	6	7	8	9	10
11	12	13	14	15	16	17
18	19	20	21	22	23	24
25	26	27	28	29	30	31

Prayer Concerns: Answers:

4 ❧ *Sunday*   *Matthew 4*

5 ❧ *Monday*   *Matthew 5:1—26*

6 ❧ *Tuesday*   *Matthew 5:27—48*

24

7 ✎ *Wednesday*

Matthew 6:1—18

8 ✎ *Thursday*

Matthew 6:19—34

9 ✎ *Friday*

Matthew 7

10 ✎ *Saturday*

Matthew 8:1—17

Paper White Narcissus

Blessed is the man who perseveres under trial, because when he has stood the test, he will receive the crown of life that God has promised to those who love him. —James 1:12

Circumstances do not make a man either strong or weak, but they show what he is. —Thomas à Kempis

JANUARY 1998

S	M	T	W	T	F	S
				1	2	3
4	5	6	7	8	9	10
11	12	13	14	15	16	17
18	19	20	21	22	23	24
25	26	27	28	29	30	31

Prayer Concerns: Answers:

11 ❧ Sunday

Matthew 8:18—34

12 ❧ Monday

Matthew 9:1—17

13 ❧ Tuesday

Matthew 9:18—38

14 ❧ *Wednesday*

Matthew 10:1—20

15 ❧ *Thursday*

Matthew 10:21—42

16 ❧ *Friday*

Matthew 11

17 ❧ *Saturday*

Matthew 12:1—23

Paper White Narcissus

Your word is a lamp to my feet
and a light for my path.
—Psalm 119:105

S	M	T	W	T	F	S
				1	2	3
4	5	6	7	8	9	10
11	12	13	14	15	16	17
18	19	20	21	22	23	24
25	26	27	28	29	30	31

Do you know a book that you are willing to put under your head for a pillow when you are dying? That is the book you want to study while you are living. There is but one such book in the world.   —Joseph Cook

Prayer Concerns: **Answers:**

18 ❦ Sunday

Matthew 12:24—50

19 ❦ Monday

Matthew 13:1—30

20 ❦ Tuesday

Matthew 13:31—58

21 ❧ Wednesday

Matthew 14:1—21

22 ❧ Thursday

Matthew 14:22—36

23 ❧ Friday

Matthew 15:1—20

24 ❧ Saturday

Matthew 15:21—39

Paper White Narcissus

Godliness with contentment is
great gain. For we brought
nothing into the world, and we can take
nothing out of it.   —1 Timothy 6:6—7

The contented man is never poor; the discontented
never rich.   —Anonymous

JANUARY 1998
S M T W T F S
          1 2 3
4 5 6 7 8 9 10
11 12 13 14 15 16 17
18 19 20 21 22 23 24
25 26 27 28 29 30 31

Prayer Concerns:

Answers:

25 ❧ *Sunday*

Matthew 16

26 ❧ *Monday*

Matthew 17

27 ❧ *Tuesday*

Matthew 18:1—20

28 ❧ *Wednesday*

Matthew 18:21—35

29 ❧ *Thursday*

Matthew 19

30 ❧ *Friday*

Matthew 20:1—16

31 ❧ *Saturday*

Matthew 20:17—34

Violet

I am the Lord your God, who
teaches you what is best for you, who
directs you in the way you should go.
—Isaiah 48:17

No man ever prayed heartily without learning something.
—Ralph Waldo Emerson

FEBRUARY 1998

S	M	T	W	T	F	S
1	2	3	4	5	6	
8	9	10	11	12	13	1
15	16	17	18	19	20	2
22	23	24	25	26	27	2

Prayer Concerns:

Answers:

1 ✎ Sunday

Matthew 21:1—22

2 ✎ Monday

Matthew 21:23—46

3 ✎ Tuesday

Matthew 22:1—22

4 ❧ *Wednesday*   *Matthew 22:23—46*

5 ❧ *Thursday*   *Matthew 23:1—22*

6 ❧ *Friday*   *Matthew 23:23—39*

7 ❧ *Saturday*   *Matthew 24:1—28*

Violet

My sheep listen to my voice; I
know them, and they follow me.
                    —John 10:27

Conversion is but the first step in the divine life. As long
as we live we should more and more be turning from all
that is evil, and to all that is good. — Tryon Edwards

FEBRUARY 1998
S M T W T F S
1 2 3 4 5 6
8 9 10 11 12 13 1
15 16 17 18 19 20 2
22 23 24 25 26 27 2

Prayer Concerns:

Answers:

8 ☙ Sunday

Matthew 24:29—51

9 ☙ Monday

Matthew 25:1—30

10 ☙ Tuesday

Matthew 25:31—46

11 ❧ *Wednesday*   *Matthew 26:1—25*

12 ❧ *Thursday*   *Matthew 26:26—50*

13 ❧ *Friday*   *Matthew 26:51—75*

14 ❧ *Saturday*   *Matthew 27:1—26*

Violet

Let us not become weary in doing good, for at the proper time we will reap a harvest if we do not give up.
—Galatians 6:9

Do all the good you can, in all the ways you can, to all the souls you can, in every place you can, at all the times you can, with all the zeal you can, as long as ever you can.
—John Wesley

FEBRUARY 1998

S	M	T	W	T	F	S
1	2	3	4	5	6	7
8	9	10	11	12	13	14
15	16	17	18	19	20	21
22	23	24	25	26	27	28

Prayer Concerns:

Answers:

15 ❧ Sunday

Matthew 27:27—50

16 ❧ Monday

Matthew 27:51—66

17 ❧ Tuesday

Matthew 28

18 ❧ *Wednesday*

Mark 1:1—22

19 ❧ *Thursday*

Mark 1:23—45

20 ❧ *Friday*

Mark 2

21 ❧ *Saturday*

Mark 3:1—19

Violet

Blessed are you when people insult
you, persecute you and falsely say all
kinds of evil against you because of me.
Rejoice and be glad, because great is your reward in heaven.
—Matthew 5:11—12

Difficulties are God's errands; and when we are sent upon
them we should esteem it a proof of God's confidence—as
a compliment from him.   —Henry Ward Beecher

FEBRUARY 1998

S	M	T	W	T	F	S
	1	2	3	4	5	6	7
8	9	10	11	12	13	14
15	16	17	18	19	20	21
22	23	24	25	26	27	28

Prayer Concerns: **Answers:**

22 ❧ Sunday   *Mark 3:20—35*

23 ❧ Monday   *Mark 4:1—20*

24 ❧ Tuesday   *Mark 4:21—41*

25 ❦ *Wednesday*

Mark 5:1—20

26 ❦ *Thursday*

Mark 5:21—43

27 ❦ *Friday*

Mark 6:1—29

28 ❦ *Saturday*

Mark 6:30—56

Hyacinth

Love one another deeply, from the heart. —1 Peter 1:22

Something the heart must have to cherish; must love, and joy, and sorrow learn: something with passion clasp, or perish, and in itself to ashes burn. —Henry Wadsworth Longfellow

MARCH 1998
S M T W T F S
1 2 3 4 5 6 7
8 9 10 11 12 13 14
15 16 17 18 19 20 21
22 23 24 25 26 27 28
29 30 31

Prayer Concerns:

Answers:

1 ❧ *Sunday*

Mark 7:1—23

2 ❧ *Monday*

Mark 7:24—37

3 ❧ *Tuesday*

Mark 8:1—21

4 ❧ *Wednesday*

Mark 8:22—38

5 ❧ *Thursday*

Mark 9:1—29

6 ❧ *Friday*

Mark 9:30—50

7 ❧ *Saturday*

Mark 10:1—31

Hyacinth

Blessed are those whose
strength is in you, who have set
their hearts on pilgrimage. . . .
They go from strength to strength, till each appears
before God in Zion. —Psalm 84:5, 7

The reward of one duty done is the power to fulfill
another. —George Eliot

MARCH 1998
S M T W T F S
1 2 3 4 5 6 7
8 9 10 11 12 13 14
15 16 17 18 19 20 21
22 23 24 25 26 27 28
29 30 31

Prayer Concerns:

Answers:

8 ❧ Sunday

Mark 10:32—52

9 ❧ Monday

Mark 11:1—18

10 ❧ Tuesday

Mark 11:19—33

1998 March

11 ❧ Wednesday

Mark 12:1—27

12 ❧ Thursday

Mark 12:28—44

13 ❧ Friday

Mark 13:1—20

14 ❧ Saturday

Mark 13:21—37

Hyacinth

In him you too are being built together to become a dwelling in which God lives by his Spirit.
—Ephesians 2:22

God did not write solo parts for very many of us. He expects us to be participants in the great symphony of life. —Donald Tippett

MARCH 1998						
S	M	T	W	T	F	S
1	2	3	4	5	6	7
8	9	10	11	12	13	14
15	16	17	18	19	20	21
22	23	24	25	26	27	28
29	30	31				

Prayer Concerns:

Answers:

15 ✽ Sunday

Mark 14:1—26

16 ✽ Monday

Mark 14:27—53

17 ✽ Tuesday

Mark 14:54—72

18 ❧ *Wednesday*

Mark 15:1—25

19 ❧ *Thursday*

Mark 15:26—47

20 ❧ *Friday*

Mark 16

21 ❧ *Saturday*

Luke 1:1—20

Hyacinth

The foolishness of God is wiser than man's wisdom, and the weakness of God is stronger than man's strength.   —1 Corinthians 1:25

The errors of faith are better than the best thoughts of unbelief.   —Thomas Russell

MARCH 1998

S	M	T	W	T	F	S
1	2	3	4	5	6	7
8	9	10	11	12	13	14
15	16	17	18	19	20	21
22	23	24	25	26	27	28
29	30	31				

Prayer Concerns:

Answers:

22 ❧ *Sunday*

Luke 1:21—38

23 ❧ *Monday*

Luke 1:39—56

24 ❧ *Tuesday*

Luke 1:57—80

46

25 ❧ Wednesday

Luke 2:1—24

26 ❧ Thursday

Luke 2:25—52

27 ❧ Friday

Luke 3

28 ❧ Saturday

Luke 4:1—30

Hyacinth

See to it that no one misses the
grace of God and that no bitter
root grows up to cause trouble
and defile many. —Hebrews 12:15

A Christian will find it cheaper to pardon than to
resent. Forgiveness saves the expense of anger, the cost
of hatred, the waste of spirits.   —Hannah More

MARCH 1998

S	M	T	W	T	F	S
1	2	3	4	5	6	7
8	9	10	11	12	13	14
15	16	17	18	19	20	21
22	23	24	25	26	27	28
29	30	31				

Prayer Concerns:

Answers:

29 • Sunday

Luke 4:31—44

30 • Monday

Luke 5:1—16

31 • Tuesday

Luke 5:17—39

1998 March

April 1 ❧ Wednesday

Luke 6:1—26

2 ❧ Thursday

Luke 6:27—49

3 ❧ Friday

Luke 7:1—30

4 ❧ Saturday

Luke 7:31—50

Tulip

Let us consider how we may spur one another on toward love and good deeds.   —Hebrews 10:24

How often have you met a critic of the church who has tried to make it better?   —Sunshine

APRIL **1998**

S	M	T	W	T	F	S
				1	2	3	4
5	6	7	8	9	10	11
12	13	14	15	16	17	18
19	20	21	22	23	24	25
26	27	28	29	30		

Prayer Concerns: **Answers:**

5 ❧ Sunday   *Luke 8:1—25*

6 ❧ Monday   *Luke 8:26—56*

7 ❧ Tuesday   *Luke 9:1—17*

50

8 ❧ *Wednesday*   *Luke 9:18—36*

9 ❧ *Thursday*   *Luke 9:37—62*

10 ❧ *Friday*   *Luke 10:1—24*

11 ❧ *Saturday*   *Luke 10:25—42*

Tulip

So then, each of us will give an account of himself to God. —Romans 14:12

The awful importance of this life is that it determines eternity. —William Barclay

APRIL **1998**

S	M	T	W	T	F	S
			1	2	3	4
5	6	7	8	9	10	11
12	13	14	15	16	17	18
19	20	21	22	23	24	25
26	27	28	29	30		

Prayer Concerns:

Answers:

12 ❧ *Sunday*

Luke 11:1—28

13 ❧ *Monday*

Luke 11:29—54

14 ❧ *Tuesday*

Luke 12:1—31

15 ❧ *Wednesday*   Luke 12:32—59

16 ❧ *Thursday*   Luke 13:1—22

17 ❧ *Friday*   Luke 13:23—35

18 ❧ *Saturday*   Luke 14:1—24

Tulip

Always give yourselves fully to the work of
the Lord, because you know that your labor in the Lord
is not in vain.   —1 Corinthians 15:58

. . . that best portion of a good man's life, his little,
nameless, unremembered acts of kindness and of love.
                              —William Wordsworth

APRIL **1998**

S	M	T	W	T	F	S
			1	2	3	4
5	6	7	8	9	10	11
12	13	14	15	16	17	18
19	20	21	22	23	24	25
26	27	28	29	30		

Prayer Concerns:

Answers:

19 ❧ *Sunday*

Luke 14:25—35

20 ❧ *Monday*

Luke 15:1—10

21 ❧ *Tuesday*

Luke 15:11—32

22 ☛ *Wednesday*   *Luke 16*

23 ☛ *Thursday*   *Luke 17:1—19*

24 ☛ *Friday*   *Luke 17:20—37*

25 ☛ *Saturday*   *Luke 18:1—23*

Tulip

Blessed are the pure in heart, for they
will see God.

—Matthew 5:8

Happiness can be built only on virtue, and must of
necessity have truth for its foundation.

—Samuel Taylor Coleridge

APRIL 1998

S	M	T	W	T	F	S
			1	2	3	4
5	6	7	8	9	10	1
12	13	14	15	16	17	18
19	20	21	22	23	24	25
26	27	28	29	30		

Prayer Concerns:

Answers:

26 ❧ *Sunday*

Luke 18:24—43

27 ❧ *Monday*

Luke 19:1—27

28 ❧ *Tuesday*

Luke 19:28—48

29 ❧ *Wednesday*

Luke 20:1—26

30 ❧ *Thursday*

Luke 20:27—47

May 1 ❧ *Friday*

Luke 21:1—19

2 ❧ *Saturday*

Luke 21:20—38

Pansy

Search me, O God, and know my heart; test me and know my anxious thoughts.   —Psalm 139:23

Suppose that a man would advertise to take photographs of the heart; would he get many customers?
      —Dwight L. Moody

MAY 1998

S M T W T F S
              1
3 4 5 6 7 8
10 11 12 13 14 15 1
17 18 19 20 21 22 2
24 25 26 27 28 29 3
31

Prayer Concerns: Answers:

3 ❧ Sunday   Luke 22:1—20

4 ❧ Monday   Luke 22:21—46

5 ❧ Tuesday   Luke 22:47—71

58

6 ❧ *Wednesday*

Luke 23:1—25

7 ❧ *Thursday*

Luke 23:26—56

8 ❧ *Friday*

Luke 24:1—35

9 ❧ *Saturday*

Luke 24:36—53

Pansy

Do not be deceived: God cannot be mocked. A man reaps what he sows.
　　　　　—Galatians 6:7

What men usually ask for when they pray to God is that two and two may not make four.
　　　　　—Russian proverb

MAY 1998

S	M	T	W	T	F	S
					1	2
3	4	5	6	7	8	9
10	11	12	13	14	15	16
17	18	19	20	21	22	23
24	25	26	27	28	29	30
31						

Prayer Concerns:

Answers:

10 ✍ Sunday

John 1:1—28

11 ✍ Monday

John 1:29—51

12 ✍ Tuesday

John 2

13 ❧ *Wednesday*   *John 3:1—18*

14 ❧ *Thursday*   *John 3:19—36*

15 ❧ *Friday*   *John 4:1—30*

16 ❧ *Saturday*   *John 4:31—54*

Pansy

Be kind and compassionate to one
another, forgiving each other, just as in
Christ God forgave you.   —Ephesians 4:32

A kind heart is a fountain of gladness, making
everything in its vicinity to freshen into smiles.
                                              —Washington Irving

MAY 1998

S	M	T	W	T	F	S
					1	2
3	4	5	6	7	8	9
10	11	12	13	14	15	16
17	18	19	20	21	22	23
24	25	26	27	28	29	30
31						

Prayer Concerns:

Answers:

17 ❧ Sunday

John 5:1—24

18 ❧ Monday

John 5:25—47

19 ❧ Tuesday

John 6:1—21

20 ❧ *Wednesday*   John 6:22—44

21 ❧ *Thursday*   John 6:45—71

22 ❧ *Friday*   John 7:1—27

23 ❧ *Saturday*   John 7:28—53

Pansy

Set your mind on things above,
not on earthly things.

—Colossians 3:2

No man will go to heaven when he dies who has not sent
his heart thither while he lives.

—Daniel Wilson

MAY 1998

S	M	T	W	T	F	S
					1	
3	4	5	6	7	8	
10	11	12	13	14	15	1
17	18	19	20	21	22	2
24	25	26	27	28	29	3
31						

Prayer Concerns:

Answers:

24 ✆ Sunday

John 8:1—27

25 ✆ Monday

John 8:28—59

26 ✆ Tuesday

John 9:1—23

27 ❧ *Wednesday*

John 9:24—41

28 ❧ *Thursday*

John 10:1—23

29 ❧ *Friday*

John 10:24—42

30 ❧ *Saturday*

John 11:1—29

Rose

Be joyful always; pray
continually; give thanks in all circumstances.
—1 Thessalonians 5:16—18

Instead of weeping when a tragedy occurs in a songbird's
life, it sings away its grief. I believe we could well follow
the pattern of our feathered friends.—Robert S. Walker

JUNE 1998

S	M	T	W	T	F	S
	1	2	3	4	5	6
7	8	9	10	11	12	13
14	15	16	17	18	19	20
21	22	23	24	25	26	27
28	29	30				

Prayer Concerns:

Answers:

May 31 ❧ *Sunday*

John 11:30—57

1 ❧ *Monday*

John 12:1—26

2 ❧ *Tuesday*

John 12:27—50

66

1998 June

3 ❧ Wednesday

John 13:1—20

4 ❧ Thursday

John 13:21—38

5 ❧ Friday

John 14

6 ❧ Saturday

John 15

Rose

A man's wisdom gives
him patience; it is to his glory to overlook
an offense.   —Proverbs 19:11

A chip on the shoulder indicates that there is wood
higher up.   —Jack Herbert

JUNE 1998

S	M	T	W	T	F	S
	1	2	3	4	5	6
7	8	9	10	11	12	13
14	15	16	17	18	19	20
21	22	23	24	25	26	27
28	29	30				

Prayer Concerns:

Answers:

7 ✈ *Sunday*

John 16

8 ✈ *Monday*

John 17

9 ✈ *Tuesday*

John 18:1—18

10 ✈ Wednesday

John 18:19—40

11 ✈ Thursday

John 19:1—22

12 ✈ Friday

John 19:23—42

13 ✈ Saturday

John 20

Rose

He who refreshes others will himself be refreshed. —Proverbs 11:25

The best way to cheer yourself is to try to cheer somebody else. —*Megiddo Message*

JUNE 1998
S M T W T F S
       1 2 3 4 5 6
7 8 9 10 11 12 13
14 15 16 17 18 19 20
21 22 23 24 25 26 27
28 29 30

Prayer Concerns:

Answers:

14 Sunday

John 21

15 Monday

Acts 1

16 Tuesday

Acts 2:1—21

17 ☙ *Wednesday*

Acts 2:22—47

18 ☙ *Thursday*

Acts 3

19 ☙ *Friday*

Acts 4:1—22

20 ☙ *Saturday*

Acts 4:23—37

Rose

I pray also that the eyes of your heart may be enlightened in order that you may know the hope to which he has called you, the riches of his glorious inheritance in the saints.

—Ephesians 1:18

If the devil could be persuaded to write a bible, he would title it, "You Only Live Once." —Sydney Harris

JUNE 1998
S M T W T F S
        1 2 3 4 5 6
 7 8 9 10 11 12 13
14 15 16 17 18 19 20
21 22 23 24 25 26 27
28 29 30

Prayer Concerns:

Answers:

21 Sunday

Acts 5:1—21

22 Monday

Acts 5:22—42

23 Tuesday

Acts 6

24 ❧ *Wednesday*

Acts 7:1—21

25 ❧ *Thursday*

Acts 7:22—43

26 ❧ *Friday*

Acts 7:44—60

27 ❧ *Saturday*

Acts 8:1—25

Rose

If we confess our sins, he is faithful and just and will forgive us our sins and purify us from all unrighteousness.

—1 John 1:9

Our God has a big eraser.　　　—Billy Zeoli

JUNE 1998

S	M	T	W	T	F	S
	1	2	3	4	5	6
7	8	9	10	11	12	13
14	15	16	17	18	19	20
21	22	23	24	25	26	27
28	29	30				

Prayer Concerns:

Answers:

28 ❧ Sunday

Acts 8:26—40

29 ❧ Monday

Acts 9:1—21

30 ❧ Tuesday

Acts 9:22—43

July 1 ❧ Wednesday

Acts 10:1—23

2 ❧ Thursday

Acts 10:24—48

3 ❧ Friday

Acts 11

4 ❧ Saturday

Acts 12

Black-Eyed Susan

Look not only to your own
interests, but also to the
interests of others. —Philippians 2:4

You can make more friends in two months by becoming
interested in other people than you can in two years by
trying to get other people interested in you.
—Dale Carnegie

JULY 1998

S	M	T	W	T	F	S
			1	2	3	4
5	6	7	8	9	10	11
12	13	14	15	16	17	18
19	20	21	22	23	24	25
26	27	28	29	30	31	

Prayer Concerns:

Answers:

5 ❧ Sunday

Acts 13:1—25

6 ❧ Monday

Acts 13:26—52

7 ❧ Tuesday

Acts 14

76

8 ❧ *Wednesday*

Acts 15:1—21

9 ❧ *Thursday*

Acts 15:22—41

10 ❧ *Friday*

Acts 16:1—21

11 ❧ *Saturday*

Acts 16:22—40

Black-Eyed Susan

If you hold to my teaching,
you are really my disciples.
Then you will know the truth, and the
truth will set you free.   —John 8:31—32

Do the truth you know, and you shall learn the truth you
need to know.   —George MacDonald

JULY 1998

S	M	T	W	T	F	S
			1	2	3	4
5	6	7	8	9	10	11
12	13	14	15	16	17	18
19	20	21	22	23	24	25
26	27	28	29	30	31	

Prayer Concerns:

Answers:

12 ❧ Sunday

Acts 17:1—15

13 ❧ Monday

Acts 17:16—34

14 ❧ Tuesday

Acts 18

78

15 ✎ *Wednesday*

Acts 19:1—20

16 ✎ *Thursday*

Acts 19:21—41

17 ✎ *Friday*

Acts 20:1—16

18 ✎ *Saturday*

Acts 20:17—38

Black-Eyed Susan

How good and pleasant it is
when brothers live together
in unity!

—Psalm 133:1

Friendship doubles our joy and divides our grief.

—Anonymous

JULY 1998

S	M	T	W	T	F	S
			1	2	3	4
5	6	7	8	9	10	11
12	13	14	15	16	17	18
19	20	21	22	23	24	25
26	27	28	29	30	31	

Prayer Concerns:

Answers:

19 ✏ *Sunday*

Acts 21:1—17

20 ✏ *Monday*

Acts 21:18—40

21 ✏ *Tuesday*

Acts 22

22 ❧ *Wednesday*

Acts 23:1—15

23 ❧ *Thursday*

Acts 23:16—35

24 ❧ *Friday*

Acts 24

25 ❧ *Saturday*

Acts 25

Black-Eyed Susan

A word aptly spoken is like apples of gold in settings of silver. —Proverbs 25:11

As the sun makes ice melt, kindness causes misunderstanding, mistrust, and hostility to evaporate.
—Albert Schweitzer

JULY 1998

S	M	T	W	T	F	S
			1	2	3	4
5	6	7	8	9	10	11
12	13	14	15	16	17	18
19	20	21	22	23	24	25
26	27	28	29	30	31	

Prayer Concerns:

Answers:

26 ❧ Sunday

Acts 26

27 ❧ Monday

Acts 27:1—26

28 ❧ Tuesday

Acts 27:27—44

29 ✍ *Wednesday*

Acts 28

30 ✍ *Thursday*

Romans 1

31 ✍ *Friday*

Romans 2

August 1 ✍ *Saturday*

Romans 3

Sunflower

Do not conform any longer to the
pattern of this world, but be
transformed by the renewing of your mind.
—Romans 12:2

The man who follows a crowd will never be followed
by a crowd.   —R. S. Donnell

AUGUST 1998
S M T W T F S
2 3 4 5 6 7 8
9 10 11 12 13 14 15
16 17 18 19 20 21 22
23 24 25 26 27 28 29
30 31

Prayer Concerns: Answers:

2 ❧ *Sunday*   *Romans 4*

3 ❧ *Monday*   *Romans 5*

4 ❧ *Tuesday*   *Romans 6*

84

1998 August

5 Wednesday

Romans 7

6 Thursday

Romans 8:1—21

7 Friday

Romans 8:22—39

8 Saturday

Romans 9:1—15

Sunflower

Pray continually.
—1 Thessalonians 5:17

In forty years I have not spent fifteen
waking minutes without thinking of Jesus.
—Charles H. Spurgeon

AUGUST 1998
S M T W T F S

2 3 4 5 6 7
9 10 11 12 13 14 1
16 17 18 19 20 21 2
23 24 25 26 27 28 2
30 31

Prayer Concerns:

Answers:

9 ❧ Sunday

Romans 9:16—33

10 ❧ Monday

Romans 10

11 ❧ Tuesday

Romans 11:1—18

12   *Wednesday*   Romans 11:19—36

13   *Thursday*   Romans 12

14   *Friday*   Romans 13

15   *Saturday*   Romans 14

Sunflower

Whoever wants to become great among you must be your servant.   —Mark 10:43

Life is a lot like tennis—the one who can serve best seldom loses.   —American Druggist

AUGUST **1998**
S M T W T F S

2 3 4 5 6 7
9 10 11 12 13 14 1
16 17 18 19 20 21 2
23 24 25 26 27 28 2
30 31

Prayer Concerns:

16 ❧ Sunday

Answers:

Romans 15:1—13

17 ❧ Monday

Romans 15:14—33

18 ❧ Tuesday

Romans 16

88

19 ❧ *Wednesday*

1 Corinthians 1

20 ❧ *Thursday*

1 Corinthians 2

21 ❧ *Friday*

1 Corinthians 3

22 ❧ *Saturday*

1 Corinthians 4

Sunflower

Cleanse me with hyssop, and I
will be clean; wash me, and I will
be whiter than snow.   —Psalm 51:7

If your life looks cloudy, maybe the windows of your soul
need washing.   —Anonymous

AUGUST 1998

S	M	T	W	T	F	S
						1
2	3	4	5	6	7	8
9	10	11	12	13	14	15
16	17	18	19	20	21	22
23	24	25	26	27	28	29
30	31					

Prayer Concerns:

Answers:

23 ❧ Sunday

1 Corinthians 5

24 ❧ Monday

1 Corinthians 6

25 ❧ Tuesday

1 Corinthians 7:1—19

26 ❧ *Wednesday*

1 Corinthians 7:20—40

27 ❧ *Thursday*

1 Corinthians 8

28 ❧ *Friday*

1 Corinthians 9

29 ❧ *Saturday*

1 Corinthians 10:1—18

Bachelor's Button

The Lord is in his holy temple; let
all the earth be silent before him.
—Habakkuk 2:20

God was smart when He made man. He made four holes
in the head for information to go in, and only one for it to
come out.
—Wallace Johnson

SEPTEMBER 1998

S	M	T	W	T	F	S
		1	2	3	4	
6	7	8	9	10	11	1
13	14	15	16	17	18	1
20	21	22	23	24	25	2
27	28	29	30			

Prayer Concerns:

Answers:

August 30 ✺ *Sunday*

1 Corinthians 10:19—33

31 ✺ *Monday*

1 Corinthians 11:1—16

1 ✺ *Tuesday*

1 Corinthians 11:17—34

1998 September

2 ❧ Wednesday

1 Corinthians 12

3 ❧ Thursday

1 Corinthians 13

4 ❧ Friday

1 Corinthians 14:1—20

5 ❧ Saturday

1 Corinthians 14:21—40

Bachelor's Button

Make every effort to keep the
unity of the Spirit through the bond of
peace.   —Ephesians 4:3

One of the marks of a mature person is the ability to
dissent without creating dissension.—Don Robinson

SEPTEMBER 1998
S M T W T F S
         1 2 3 4
6 7 8 9 10 11 1
13 14 15 16 17 18 1
20 21 22 23 24 25 2
27 28 29 30

Prayer Concerns:

6 ❧ Sunday

Answers:

1 Corinthians 15:1—28

7 ❧ Monday

1 Corinthians 15:29—58

8 ❧ Tuesday

1 Corinthians 16

9 ☙ Wednesday

2 Corinthians 1

10 ☙ Thursday

2 Corinthians 2

11 ☙ Friday

2 Corinthians 3

12 ☙ Saturday

2 Corinthians 4

Bachelor's Button

The love of money is a root of all kinds of evil. Some people, eager for money, have wandered from the faith and pierced themselves with many griefs.

—1 Timothy 6:10

If a person gets his attitude toward money straight, it will help straighten out almost every other area in his life.

—Billy Graham

SEPTEMBER 199

S	M	T	W	T	F	
			1	2	3	4
6	7	8	9	10	11	
13	14	15	16	17	18	
20	21	22	23	24	25	
27	28	29	30			

Prayer Concerns:

Answers:

13 ❧ Sunday

2 Corinthians 5

14 ❧ Monday

2 Corinthians 6

15 ❧ Tuesday

2 Corinthians 7

16 ❧ *Wednesday*

2 Corinthians 8

17 ❧ *Thursday*

2 Corinthians 9

18 ❧ *Friday*

2 Corinthians 10

19 ❧ *Saturday*

2 Corinthians 11:1—15

Bachelor's Button

My God will meet all your needs according to his glorious riches in Christ Jesus.

—Philippians 4:19

Give all to God, take all from God, and use all for God.

—F. B. Meyer

SEPTEMBER 1998

S	M	T	W	T	F	S
		1	2	3	4	5
6	7	8	9	10	11	12
13	14	15	16	17	18	19
20	21	22	23	24	25	26
27	28	29	30			

Prayer Concerns:

Answers:

20 ❧ *Sunday*

2 Corinthians 11:16—33

21 ❧ *Monday*

2 Corinthians 12

22 ❧ *Tuesday*

2 Corinthians 13

98

23 ☙ *Wednesday*

Galatians 1

24 ☙ *Thursday*

Galatians 2

25 ☙ *Friday*

Galatians 3

26 ☙ *Saturday*

Galatians 4

Bachelor's Button

God demonstrates his own love for us in this: While we were still sinners, Christ died for us.

—Romans 5:8

There is no way under the sun of making a man worthy of love, except by loving him. —Thomas Merton

SEPTEMBER 1998

S	M	T	W	T	F	S
		1	2	3	4	5
6	7	8	9	10	11	12
13	14	15	16	17	18	19
20	21	22	23	24	25	26
27	28	29	30			

Prayer Concerns:

Answers:

27 ✎ *Sunday*

Galatians 5

28 ✎ *Monday*

Galatians 6

29 ✎ *Tuesday*

Ephesians 1

30 ❧ *Wednesday*

Ephesians 2

October 1 ❧ *Thursday*

Ephesians 3

2 ❧ *Friday*

Ephesians 4

3 ❧ *Saturday*

Ephesians 5:1—16

Chrysanthemum

Seek the Lord while he may
be found; call on him while he is
near.   —Isaiah 55:6

If a man wants God to leave him alone, that is what will
happen—forever.   —M. P. Horban

OCTOBER **1998**

S	M	T	W	T	F	S
				1	2	
4	5	6	7	8	9	10
11	12	13	14	15	16	1
18	19	20	21	22	23	2
25	26	27	28	29	30	3

Prayer Concerns:

Answers:

4 ❧ Sunday

Ephesians 5:17—33

5 ❧ Monday

Ephesians 6

6 ❧ Tuesday

Philippians 1

102

7 ❧ Wednesday

Philippians 2

8 ❧ Thursday

Philippians 3

9 ❧ Friday

Philippians 4

10 ❧ Saturday

Colossians 1

Chrysanthemum

Our light and momentary
troubles are achieving for us an
eternal glory that far outweighs them all.
—2 Corinthians 4:17

Adversity is God's university.   —Paul Evans

OCTOBER **1998**

S	M	T	W	T	F	S
				1	2	3
4	5	6	7	8	9	10
11	12	13	14	15	16	17
18	19	20	21	22	23	24
25	26	27	28	29	30	31

Prayer Concerns:

Answers:

11 ❧ *Sunday*

Colossians 2

12 ❧ *Monday*

Colossians 3

13 ❧ *Tuesday*

Colossians 4

14 ❧ *Wednesday*

1 Thessalonians 1

15 ❧ *Thursday*

1 Thessalonians 2

16 ❧ *Friday*

1 Thessalonians 3

17 ❧ *Saturday*

1 Thessalonians 4

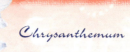

Chrysanthemum

Jesus often withdrew to
lonely places and prayed.
—Luke 5:16

You must talk to God about people before you talk to
people about God. —C. E. Prosser

OCTOBER 1998

S	M	T	W	T	F	S
				1	2	3
4	5	6	7	8	9	10
11	12	13	14	15	16	17
18	19	20	21	22	23	24
25	26	27	28	29	30	31

Prayer Concerns:

Answers:

18 Sunday

1 Thessalonians 5

19 Monday

2 Thessalonians 1

20 Tuesday

2 Thessalonians 2

106

21 ❧ Wednesday

2 Thessalonians 3

22 ❧ Thursday

1 Timothy 1

23 ❧ Friday

1 Timothy 2

24 ❧ Saturday

1 Timothy 3

Chrysanthemum

Although they knew God,
they neither glorified him as
God nor gave thanks to him.
　　　　　　—Romans 1:21

The beginning of men's rebellion against God was, and
is, the lack of a thankful heart.　—Francis Schaeffer

OCTOBER 1998

S	M	T	W	T	F	S
				1	2	3
4	5	6	7	8	9	10
11	12	13	14	15	16	17
18	19	20	21	22	23	24
25	26	27	28	29	30	31

Prayer Concerns:

Answers:

25 ✎ Sunday

1 Timothy 4

26 ✎ Monday

1 Timothy 5

27 ✎ Tuesday

1 Timothy 6

1998 October

28 Wednesday	2 Timothy 1
29 Thursday	2 Timothy 2
30 Friday	2 Timothy 3
31 Saturday	2 Timothy 4

Strawflower

I urge you, brothers, in view of
God's mercy, to offer your bodies as
living sacrifices, holy and pleasing to God.
—Romans 12:1

The altar is not a bargain counter where you haggle with
God. With Him it is all or nothing. —Lance Zavitz

NOVEMBER 1998

S	M	T	W	T	F	S
1	2	3	4	5	6	7
8	9	10	11	12	13	14
15	16	17	18	19	20	21
22	23	24	25	26	27	28
29	30					

Prayer Concerns:

Answers:

1 ❧ *Sunday*

Titus 1

2 ❧ *Monday*

Titus 2

3 ❧ *Tuesday*

Titus 3

1998 November

4 Wednesday	Philemon
5 Thursday	Hebrews 1
6 Friday	Hebrews 2
7 Saturday	Hebrews 3

Strawflower

You will seek me and find me
when you seek me with all your
heart. —Jeremiah 29:13

Sinners cannot find God for the same reason that
criminals cannot find a policeman: They aren't looking!
  —Billy Sunday

NOVEMBER 1998

S	M	T	W	T	F	S
1	2	3	4	5	6	7
8	9	10	11	12	13	14
15	16	17	18	19	20	21
22	23	24	25	26	27	28
29	30					

Prayer Concerns:

8 • Sunday

9 • Monday

10 • Tuesday

Answers:

Hebrews 4

Hebrews 5

Hebrews 6

11 ✎ *Wednesday*

Hebrews 7

12 ✎ *Thursday*

Hebrews 8

13 ✎ *Friday*

Hebrews 9

14 ✎ *Saturday*

Hebrews 10:1—18

Strawflower

Love the Lord your God with
all your heart and with all your
soul and with all your strength.
—Deuteronomy 6:5

I want my religion like my tea; I want it hot!
—William Booth

NOVEMBER **1998**

S	M	T	W	T	F	S
1	2	3	4	5	6	7
8	9	10	11	12	13	14
15	16	17	18	19	20	21
22	23	24	25	26	27	28
29	30					

Prayer Concerns:

Answers:

15 • Sunday

Hebrews 10:19—39

16 • Monday

Hebrews 11

17 • Tuesday

Hebrews 12

1998 November

18 ❧ Wednesday | Hebrews 13

19 ❧ Thursday | James 1

20 ❧ Friday | James 2

21 ❧ Saturday | James 3

Strawflower

The path of the righteous is like
the first gleam of dawn, shining
ever brighter till the full light of day.
—Proverbs 4:18

The future is as bright as the promises of God.
—Adoniram Judson

NOVEMBER 1998
S M T W T F S
1 2 3 4 5 6 7
8 9 10 11 12 13 14
15 16 17 18 19 20 21
22 23 24 25 26 27 28
29 30

Prayer Concerns: **Answers:**

22 ❧ *Sunday*   *James 4*

23 ❧ *Monday*   *James 5*

24 ❧ *Tuesday*   *1 Peter 1*

1998 November

25 ☞ Wednesday

1 Peter 2

26 ☞ Thursday

1 Peter 3

27 ☞ Friday

1 Peter 4

28 ☞ Saturday

1 Peter 5

Poinsettia

Will you not revive us again,
that your people may rejoice in
you?   —Psalm 85:6

A religious revival is nothing else than a new beginning
of obedience to God.   —Charles G. Finney

DECEMBER 1998
S M T W T F S
        1 2 3 4 5
6 7 8 9 10 11 12
13 14 15 16 17 18 19
20 21 22 23 24 25 26
27 28 29 30 31

Prayer Concerns:

November 29 ❧ Sunday

Answers:

2 Peter 1

30 ❧ Monday

2 Peter 2

1 ❧ Tuesday

2 Peter 3

118

2 ❧ Wednesday

1 John 1

3 ❧ Thursday

1 John 2

4 ❧ Friday

1 John 3

5 ❧ Saturday

1 John 4

Poinsettia

Like newborn babies, crave
pure spiritual milk, so that by it
you may grow up in your
salvation, now that you have
tasted that the Lord is good.   —1 Peter 2:2—3

The less the Bible is read, the more it's translated.
                                        —C. S. Lewis

DECEMBER 1998
S M T W T F S
        1 2 3 4
6 7 8 9 10 11 1
13 14 15 16 17 18 1
20 21 22 23 24 25 2
27 28 29 30 31

Prayer Concerns: Answers:

6 ❧ Sunday   1 John 5

7 ❧ Monday   2 John

8 ❧ Tuesday   3 John

120

1998 December

9 Wednesday

Jude

10 Thursday

Revelation 1

11 Friday

Revelation 2

12 Saturday

Revelation 3

Poinsettia

No man has power over the wind
to contain it; so no one has power
over the day of his death.
—Ecclesiastes 8:8

Death is an offer we can't refuse. —Robert M. Fine

DECEMBER 1998
S M T W T F S
      1 2 3 4 5
6 7 8 9 10 11 1*
13 14 15 16 17 18 1*
20 21 22 23 24 25 2*
27 28 29 30 31

Prayer Concerns:

Answers:

13 ❧ *Sunday*

Revelation 4

14 ❧ *Monday*

Revelation 5

15 ❧ *Tuesday*

Revelation 6

16 ❧ *Wednesday*

Revelation 7

17 ❧ *Thursday*

Revelation 8

18 ❧ *Friday*

Revelation 9

19 ❧ *Saturday*

Revelation 10

Poinsettia

One thing I ask of the Lord, this
is what I seek: that I may dwell in
the house of the Lord all the days of
my life, to gaze upon the beauty of
the Lord and to seek him in his temple. —Psalm 27:4

We are often so caught up in our activities that we tend to
worship our work, work at our play and play at our worship.
—Charles Swindoll

DECEMBER 1998

S	M	T	W	T	F	S
		1	2	3	4	5
6	7	8	9	10	11	12
13	14	15	16	17	18	19
20	21	22	23	24	25	26
27	28	29	30	31		

Prayer Concerns:

Answers:

20 ❧ Sunday

Revelation 11

21 ❧ Monday

Revelation 12

22 ❧ Tuesday

Revelation 13

23 ❧ *Wednesday*

Revelation 14

24 ❧ *Thursday*

Revelation 15

25 ❧ *Friday*

Revelation 16

26 ❧ *Saturday*

Revelation 17

Poinsettia

Do not be anxious about anything, but in everything, by prayer and petition, with thanksgiving, present your requests to God.

—Philippians 4:6

Worry is the interest paid by those who borrow trouble.

—George Lyons

DECEMBER 1998

S	M	T	W	T	F	S
		1	2	3	4	
6	7	8	9	10	11	1
13	14	15	16	17	18	1
20	21	22	23	24	25	2
27	28	29	30	31		

Prayer Concerns:

Answers:

27 ❧ *Sunday*

Revelation 18

28 ❧ *Monday*

Revelation 19

29 ❧ *Tuesday*

Revelation 20

126

30 ❧ *Wednesday*

Revelation 21

31 ❧ *Thursday*

Revelation 22

January 1 ❧ *Friday*

2 ❧ *Saturday*

Prayer Concerns Around the World

Armenia

Population: 3,470,000

Capital: Yerevan

Language: Armenian*

Literacy: 100%

Income per capita: $2,300

Religions: Orthodox 79%,
   nonreligious 17%, Muslim 3% **

Armenia is one of several former Soviet
republics struggling for freedom and prosperity amid ongoing conflict and hardship.
Devastated by a Muslim-led genocide in 1915, this historically Christian nation
today keeps a watchful eye on its Muslim neighbors. PRAY that Christians in
Armenia's state church and its growing evangelical churches will faithfully proclaim the gospel.

Australia

Population: 18,270,000

Capital: Canberra

Language: English

Literacy: 100%

Income per capita: $20,700

Religions: nonreligious 27%, Anglican 26%, non-
   Anglican Protestant 24%, Roman Catholic 20%

Even as **Australia** continues to prosper economically, its church membership roles
decline. PRAY for revival. Pray for effective outreach to the many foreign nationals
who have come to Australia in search of work, or as refugees from Vietnam and the
former Yugoslavia. Pray that Australians would have a greater vision for taking the
gospel throughout Asia.

*Where multiple languages are spoken, only the one or two most predominant are reported.
**Figures for all statistical categories are based on a comparison of several sources (see page 176) and will
   vary in accuracy. Percentages less than 1% are not reported.

Austria

Population: 8,000,000

Capital: Vienna

Language: German

Literacy: 98%

Income per capita: $19,400

Religions: Roman Catholic 83%, nonreligious 8%,
Protestant 5%, Muslim 1%

Maintaining its strict policy of neutrality,
Austria continues to play a key role in promoting political reconciliation and economic cooperation among the nations of a Europe until recently divided by the iron curtain. Though evangelical churches have grown slowly, there has been good response to evangelistic efforts. PRAY for the progress of the gospel in this strategic nation.

Bangladesh

Population: 123,070,000

Capital: Dhaka

Language: Bangla, English

Literacy: 36%

Income per capita: $1,000

Religions: Muslim 87%, Hindu 11%, Buddhist 1%

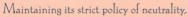

Long one of the world's most impoverished nations, **Bangladesh** has recently made strides toward greater self-sufficiency. Yet with so much of its economy based on agriculture, it remains vulnerable to recurrent natural disasters. It is one of the least evangelized nations, but church leaders are reporting an increasing response to the gospel. PRAY that this trend will continue.

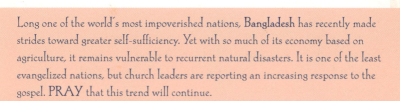

Barbados

Population: 260,000

Capital: Bridgetown

Language: English

Literacy: 99%

Income per capita: $9,200

Religions: Anglican 69%, Protestant 19%,
   nonreligious 7%, Roman Catholic 4%

The Caribbean nation of **Barbados**, comprised of just
one small island, prospers on light industry, sugar cane, and
tourism. There is little spiritual life in the nation's centuries-
old churches, the crime rate is increasing, and three-fourths of all
births are illegitimate. PRAY for spiritual revival, especially among the
youth.

Belarus

Population: 10,420,000

Capital: Minsk

Language: Belarusian, Russian

Literacy: 100%

Income per capita: $5,100

Religions: Orthodox 75%, Roman
   Catholic 20%

As the former Soviet republic of **Belarus** seeks greater prosperity, it continues to
deal with the lingering results of the Chernobyl nuclear disaster in neighboring
Ukraine—including a one-hundred-fold increase in cancer among its children.
Thank God that Belarus is seeing a great religious revival, and PRAY that the
revival will grow and produce lasting fruit.

Benin

Population: 5,710,000

Capital: Cotonou

Language: French

Literacy: 23%

Income per capita: $1,300

Religions: indigenous 55%, Roman Catholic 22%,
Muslim 17%, Protestant 4%

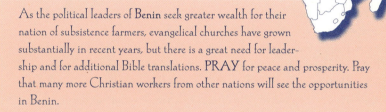

As the political leaders of **Benin** seek greater wealth for their
nation of subsistence farmers, evangelical churches have grown
substantially in recent years, but there is a great need for leadership and for additional Bible translations. PRAY for peace and prosperity. Pray
that many more Christian workers from other nations will see the opportunities
in Benin.

Bolivia

Population: 7,170,000

Capital: La Paz

Language: Spanish, Quechua

Literacy: 78%

Income per capita: $2,400

Religions: Roman Catholic 65%, indigenous 15%, Protestant 9%,
nonreligious 6%, Baha'i 3%

With its vast mineral wealth, **Bolivia** was once the richest
nation in South America. Today, due to the worldwide col-
lapse of tin prices, it is the poorest, depending mainly on agricultural exports. Economic hardship has, however, drawn many to faith in Christ.
PRAY for a continued strong response to the gospel, and for ongoing efforts to
reach the remote Quechua Indians with radio broadcasts in their language.

133

Bosnia and Herzegovina

Population: 2,660,000
Capital: Sarajevo
Language: Bosnian
Literacy: 86%
Income per capita: $3,200
Religions: Muslim 40%, Orthodox 28%,
   Roman Catholic 14%,
   nonreligious 13%, Protestant 4%

As **Bosnia and Herzegovina** seeks a permanent end to war, there are concerns that the Iranians who have helped them in wartime will succeed in bringing their brand of militant Islam to the region. PRAY for a lasting peace, and that the plans of Muslim conquest will be answered by true ethnic reconciliation and an effective gospel outreach. Pray for the well-being and salvation of the hundreds of thousands who have fled their homeland.

Botswana

Population: 1,480,000
Capital: Gaborone
Language: English, Setswana
Literacy: 72%
Income per capita: $3,100
Religions: indigenous 37%, indigenous Christian 35%,
   Protestant 20%, Roman Catholic 7%

Botswana is a rare success story in the history of foreign aid: Now essentially self-sufficient, it recently hosted a dinner in Washington to thank the United States for past assistance. While most of the people are nominally Christian, there is little true commitment, many churches mix Christianity with ancient tribal religions, and 90 percent of births are illegitimate. PRAY for a nationwide spiritual renewal.

Brazil

Population: 162,660,000

Capital: Brasília

Language: Portuguese

Literacy: 81%

Income per capita: $4,300

Religions: Roman Catholic 68%, Protestant 22%, indigenous 5%, nonreligious 2%

Brazil is rich in natural resources and is perhaps the world's leading producer of coffee and exporter of iron ore. Yet more than half of its people are malnourished. Christianity has flourished. Thank God for the many new believers, and PRAY for their physical and spiritual well-being. Pray especially for the success of ministries among the hundreds of thousands of homeless children in large cities.

Burkina Faso

Population: 10,620,000

Capital: Ouagadougou

Language: French

Literacy: 18%

Income per capita: $660

Religions: Muslim 47%, indigenous 33%, Roman Catholic 14%, Protestant 5%

Most of Burkina Faso's people are farmers or cattle herders, yet the encroaching Sahara Desert threatens their livelihood; much of the nation's food comes from imports and foreign aid. There has been strong response to the gospel in recent years, even in the Muslim areas of the north. Praise God for these new believers, and PRAY for ministries such as radio and video presentations, vital in a land where few can read.

Canada

Population: 29,860,000
Capital: Ottawa
Language: English, French
Literacy: 99%
Income per capita: $19,200
Religions: Roman Catholic 45%,
   non-Anglican Protestant 31%, Anglican 10%,
   nonreligious 7%, Orthodox 2%, Jewish 1%

With rich mineral reserves, a solid industrial base, and vast prairies that provide one-fifth of the world's wheat, **Canada** continues to prosper even amid ongoing concerns about a break between French-speaking Quebec and the other nine provinces, where English is the primary language. PRAY for Canada's survival as one nation, and pray for revival in its churches, especially among the native people groups of the far north.

Cape Verde

Population: 450,000
Capital: Praia
Language: Portuguese, Creole
Literacy: 66%
Income per capita: $1,000
Religions: Roman Catholic 95%, Protestant 3%

The mountainous **Cape Verde** Islands, 400 miles west of Africa, suffer from lack of farmland and the lingering results of socialist planning. While many of the people make a living from fishing, most income is from islanders who earn their living abroad. The Roman Catholic majority is mostly nominal and often superstitious in faith. PRAY for more Christian literature in the Creole spoken by most Caboverdians.

People's Republic of China (mainland)

Population: 1,210,000,000

Capital: Beijing

Language: Chinese

Literacy: 78%

Income per capita: $2,500

Religions: nonreligious 57%, indigenous 28%, Protestant 6%, Muslim 3%, Buddhist 3%

The officially communist **People's Republic of China** has in recent years heard its leaders say that "to get rich is glorious." China has also heard the far more glorious message of eternal salvation through Jesus Christ. Though religious persecution continues, China's churches continue to grow and its printing presses produce more than 2 million Bibles per year. PRAY for the progress of the gospel in this largest nation of the world.

Republic of China (Taiwan)

Population: 21,300,000

Capital: Taipei

Language: Chinese

Literacy: 94%

Income per capita: $12,400

Religions: indigenous/Buddhist 70%, nonreligious 24%, Protestant 3%, Roman Catholic 2%

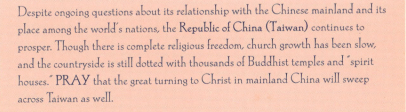

Despite ongoing questions about its relationship with the Chinese mainland and its place among the world's nations, the **Republic of China (Taiwan)** continues to prosper. Though there is complete religious freedom, church growth has been slow, and the countryside is still dotted with thousands of Buddhist temples and "spirit houses." PRAY that the great turning to Christ in mainland China will sweep across Taiwan as well.

Colombia

Population: 36,810,000
Capital: Bogotá
Language: Spanish
Literacy: 91%
Income per capita: $4,900
Religions: Roman Catholic 93%, Protestant 5%, indigenous 1%

Efforts to rid **Colombia** of the scourge of drug cultivation and marketing are perennially hampered by the involvement of government officials and other key society leaders in the drug trade. Meanwhile, evangelical churches continue to grow despite the ongoing persecution of Bible translators. PRAY that the difficulties faced by Colombian Christians will be a source of strength rather than a discouragement.

Comoros

Population: 570,000
Capital: Moroni
Language: Arabic, French
Literacy: 48%
Income per capita: $700
Religions: Muslim 86%, Roman Catholic 13%

Politically turbulent since independence from France in 1975, the **Comoro** Islands also suffer from overpopulation, high unemployment, and an insufficient food supply. The primary local faith—a combination of Islam and spiritism—has proven resistant to the gospel. The few evangelical Christians have often been persecuted. PRAY that these Christians will remain committed to practicing and sharing their faith.

Costa Rica

Population: 3,460,000

Capital: San José

Language: Spanish

Literacy: 93%

Income per capita: $5,100

Religions: Roman Catholic 80%, Protestant 11%, nonreligious 6%

With a constitution forbidding it to have an army, **Costa Rica** has been a haven of prosperity and stability amid the turmoil of Central America and northern South America. Its wealth comes mostly from agriculture, but its industrial base is growing fast. There has been a great response to the gospel, but a high percentage of those responding have not remained faithful. PRAY for mature, committed leaders to disciple new believers.

Cuba

Population: 11,000,000

Capital: Havana

Language: Spanish

Literacy: 94%

Income per capita: $1,300

Religions: Roman Catholic 41%, nonreligious 31%, indigenous 24%, Protestant 3%

Despite renewed persecution, the church in **Cuba** continues to grow—through evangelistic efforts and through the house church movement. Perhaps as many as a million Cubans identify with evangelical churches. PRAY that the years ahead will bring greater freedom and prosperity to Cuba, and that Cuba's churches will prosper as well.

Czech Republic

Population: 10,300,000

Capital: Prague

Language: Czech

Literacy: 99%

Income per capita: $7,400

Religions: Roman Catholic 63%, nonreligious 27%, Protestant 6%, other Catholic 3%

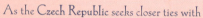

As the Czech Republic seeks closer ties with
Western Europe, it brings to that new alliance the economic might
that once made it so valuable an ally to the Soviet Union. Communism was very
successful in undermining the nation's Christian heritage, and few Czechs today
would consider themselves evangelical in faith. PRAY for good Christian literature
aimed at young Czechs seeking their way in a post-communist world.

Djibouti

Population: 430,000

Capital: Djibouti

Language: Arabic, Afar

Literacy: 48%

Income per capita: $1,200

Religions: Muslim 95%, Roman Catholic 4%

Djibouti is perennially plagued by drought, lack of natural resources,
civil strife, and 50 percent unemployment. There are few Christians in this Muslim
land, where conversion can mean becoming a social outcast. The New Testament
was recently translated and published in the Afar language, which half of the people speak. PRAY that this new translation will encourage believers and lead many
more into God's kingdom.

Dominican Republic

Population: 8,100,000

Capital: Santo Domingo

Language: Spanish, English

Literacy: 74%

Income per capita: $3,100

Religions: Roman Catholic 91%, Protestant 6%

The **Dominican Republic**, which shares the mountainous island of Hispaniola with Haiti, enjoys a per capita income four times as high as that of its impoverished neighbor. Yet with 30 percent unemployment, it faces economic challenges of its own. PRAY that the steady church growth of recent years will continue. Pray for better treatment for the Haitians—many of whom are Christians—who work in Dominican sugar cane fields.

Egypt

Population: 63,600,000

Capital: Cairo

Language: Arabic

Literacy: 50%

Income per capita: $2,500

Religions: Muslim 85%, Orthodox 13%, Protestant 1%

Muslim fundamentalists in **Egypt** are waging cultural warfare against all Western influences, including Christianity. Their tactics include banning "un-Islamic" books, terrorism against tourists, and demanding "protection money" from Christian farmers. Christians in general are seldom free from the fear of persecution. PRAY for the safety and faithful witness of Egyptian Christians.

Equatorial Guinea

Population: 430,000
Capital: Malabo
Language: Spanish, pidgin English
Literacy: 50%
Income per capita: $700
Religions: Roman Catholic 88%, Protestant 5%, indigenous 5%

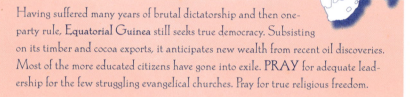

Having suffered many years of brutal dictatorship and then one-party rule, **Equatorial Guinea** still seeks true democracy. Subsisting on its timber and cocoa exports, it anticipates new wealth from recent oil discoveries. Most of the more educated citizens have gone into exile. PRAY for adequate leadership for the few struggling evangelical churches. Pray for true religious freedom.

Eritrea

Population: 3,910,000
Capital: Asmara
Language: Arabic, Tigrinya
Literacy: 20%
Income per capita: $500
Religions: Muslim 51%, Orthodox 40%, Catholic 4%, nonreligious 3%, Protestant 2%

Forcibly incorporated into Ethiopia in 1952, **Eritrea** declared its independence in 1993. Still impoverished, Eritrea has improved its agricultural output and is working to develop its oil resources and promote tourism on its long Red Sea coast. PRAY that churches devastated by Ethiopian Marxists will once again flourish. Pray that many who became Christians while exiled to Sudan will be able to return and will strengthen the church.

Ethiopia

Population: 57,170,000

Capital: Addis Ababa

Language: Amharic, English

Literacy: 33%

Income per capita: $380

Religions: Orthodox 43%, Muslim 35%, Protestant 14%, indigenous 6%

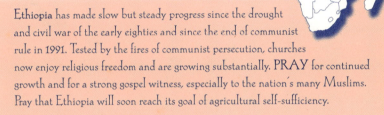

Ethiopia has made slow but steady progress since the drought and civil war of the early eighties and since the end of communist rule in 1991. Tested by the fires of communist persecution, churches now enjoy religious freedom and are growing substantially. PRAY for continued growth and for a strong gospel witness, especially to the nation's many Muslims. Pray that Ethiopia will soon reach its goal of agricultural self-sufficiency.

France

Population: 58,320,000

Capital: Paris

Language: French

Literacy: 99%

Income per capita: $26,200

Religions: Roman Catholic 68%, nonreligious 19%, Muslim 8%, Protestant 2%

Like other wealthy European nations, France seeks to maintain its high living standards and generous welfare system while staying competitive in an expanding world economy. French truck drivers recently blockaded roads to press their demand for a retirement age of 55! Meanwhile, France is listed along with developing nations as being among the least evangelized. PRAY that France will once again turn to Christ.

Gabon

Population: 1,170,000
Capital: Libreville
Language: French, Bantu
Literacy: 95%
Income per capita: $3,600
Religions: Roman Catholic 55%, Protestant 18%,
  indigenous Christian 14%, indigenous 6%, Muslim 4%

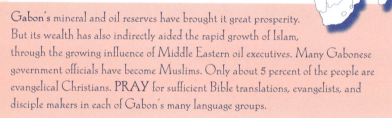

Gabon's mineral and oil reserves have brought it great prosperity. But its wealth has also indirectly aided the rapid growth of Islam, through the growing influence of Middle Eastern oil executives. Many Gabonese government officials have become Muslims. Only about 5 percent of the people are evangelical Christians. PRAY for sufficient Bible translations, evangelists, and disciple makers in each of Gabon's many language groups.

Germany

Population: 83,540,000
Capital: Berlin
Language: German
Literacy: 98%
Income per capita: $28,300 (average of East and
  West)
Religions: Protestant 37%, Roman Catholic 36%,
  nonreligious 21%, Muslim 2%

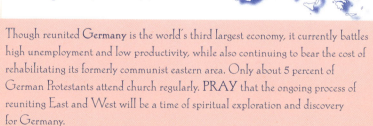

Though reunited Germany is the world's third largest economy, it currently battles high unemployment and low productivity, while also continuing to bear the cost of rehabilitating its formerly communist eastern area. Only about 5 percent of German Protestants attend church regularly. PRAY that the ongoing process of reuniting East and West will be a time of spiritual exploration and discovery for Germany.

Ghana

Population: 17,700,000

Capital: Accra

Language: English

Literacy: 60%

Income per capita: $1,300

Religions: Protestant 28%, indigenous 20%, Roman Catholic 19%,
indigenous Christian 16%, Muslim 16%

Ghana is one of the world's main producers of cocoa, and it has vast resources of oil, gold, and timber, but years of economic mismanagement have left it relatively poor. Two-thirds of all Ghanians claim a Christian heritage, but only about a tenth attend church regularly. PRAY that the revivals of recent years will have a lasting impact, especially on the largely unreached northern people groups.

Greece

Population: 10,720,000

Capital: Athens

Language: Greek

Literacy: 93%

Income per capita: $8,900

Religions: Orthodox 97%, Muslim 1%

The people of **Greece**, a mountainous land with more than 150 inhabited islands, make their living from tourism, shipping, and farming. The former Yugoslavia is Greece's main connection to the rest of Europe, and the recent fighting in that region has meant economic hardship for Greece. Though most Greeks claim to be Christians, only 2 percent attend church and evangelicals are often persecuted. PRAY for a courageous gospel witness.

Guatemala

Population: 11,280,000

Capital: Guatemala City

Language: Spanish

Literacy: 55%

Income per capita: $3,100

Religions: Roman Catholic 71%, Protestant 26%

Guatemala's decades-long civil war with Marxist rebels came to an official end late in 1996. Many observers credit the country's fast-growing evangelical churches with helping foster the atmosphere in which such a truce could occur. PRAY that peace will last; pray that Guatemala will recover from the devastation of many years of fighting. Pray that Guatemalans will continue finding eternal peace and salvation in Christ.

Guinea

Population: 7,410,000

Capital: Conakry

Language: French

Literacy: 24% in French, 48% in tribal languages

Income per capita: $980

Religions: Muslim 83%, indigenous 12%, Roman Catholic 4%

Though having vast reserves of gold, diamonds, iron ore, and bauxite, and rich farmland as well, because of mismanagement and corruption Guinea remains poor and imports much of its food. Less than 1 percent of Guineans are evangelical Christians. Since 1984—after years of Marxist and Muslim persecution—they have been free to evangelize. PRAY for a harvest of souls, especially among Muslims, who have been more open in recent years.

Haiti

Population: 6,730,000
Capital: Port-au-Prince
Language: French, Creole
Literacy: 25%
Income per capita: $870
Religions: Roman Catholic 72%, Protestant 25%

Despite the return of democracy and the resulting end of economic sanctions, Haiti remains the most impoverished of Western nations. Christian ministries struggle to help amid the constant threats of crime and disease. PRAY for a workable solution to Haiti's poverty, and that the truth of the gospel will win out over the spiritism and witchcraft practiced by most Haitians.

India

Population: 952,110,000
Capital: New Delhi
Language: Hindi, English
Literacy: 52%
Income per capita: $1,300
Religions: Hindu 79%, Muslim 12%,
   Roman Catholic 2%, Protestant 2%, Sikh 2%

While India remains primarily non-Christian and closed to outside missions, indigenous Christian ministries are seeing an increasing response to the gospel. PRAY for these faithful servants of Christ, who proclaim the gospel amid a rising tide of Hindu nationalism. Pray that many Hindus, who claim to accept all religions equally, will realize that Jesus is the only way to true, eternal salvation.

Indonesia

Population: 206,610,000
Capital: Jakarta
Language: Indonesian
Literacy: 86%
Income per capita: $3,100
Religions: Muslim 78%, Protestant 11%,
Roman Catholic 3%, Hindu 3%, Buddhist 2%

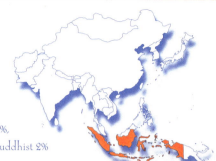

Indonesia has grown prosperous in recent years, though that prosperity is tainted by increasing levels of government corruption. Despite persecution from both the government and Muslim fundamentalists, evangelical Christianity is prospering as well. PRAY for good leadership for these churches filled largely with first-generation believers. Pray for Bible translators for the nation's 500 language groups.

Iran

Population: 66,100,000
Capital: Teheran
Language: Farsi
Literacy: 74%
Income per capita: $4,720
Religions: Muslim 98%, Orthodox 1%,
Zoroastrian 1%

Though Iran has suffered economically in recent years because of widespread boycotts of its oil industry, it continues to support terrorism abroad and to wage holy war against Christians within its own borders. Muslim fundamentalists consider conversion by Muslims to Christianity a capital offense, and they have killed many such converts. PRAY for courage for the estimated 15,000 Christians in Iran.

Iraq

Population: 21,420,000
Capital: Baghdad
Language: Arabic
Literacy: 60%
Income per capita: $2,000
Religions: Muslim 95%, Christian 4%

Iraq has been in recent years politically and economically isolated from much of the world, as it pursues strongly anti-Israel policies and periodically threatens its neighbors. Only a tiny fraction of 1 percent of Iraqis claim a saving faith in Christ. PRAY for the few faithful Iraqi pastors who study Bible correspondence courses in secret in order to better lead their flocks. Pray for more peace-loving political leaders.

Israel

Population: 5,220,000
Capital: Jerusalem
Language: Hebrew, Arabic
Literacy: 92%
Income per capita: $13,900
Religions: Jewish 80%, Muslim 15%, Druze 2%,
    Roman Catholic 1%

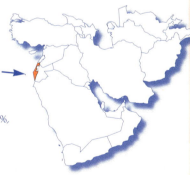

As Israel continues to fight for its existence amid the predominantly Muslim Middle East, a very small but steadily increasing number of Israelis are recognizing Christ as their true Messiah and their only real hope for peace. PRAY for these Christians who, when they dare to witness openly, face hostility on all sides. Pray that the uncertainty of life in this region will turn many more Israelis to Christ.

Italy
Population: 57,460,000
Capital: Rome
Language: Italian
Literacy: 97%
Income per capita: $17,200
Religions: Roman Catholic 78%,
    nonreligious 18%, Muslim 2%, Protestant 1%

With organized crime permeating all of society, including politics, **Italy** has had 50 new governments since World War II. Meanwhile the Catholic Church, Italy's greatest unifying factor, steadily loses members and influence. Evangelical churches are small but growing steadily, with significant recent responses to gospel crusades. PRAY that more and more Italians will find their true identity in Jesus Christ.

Japan
Population: 125,570,000
Capital: Tokyo
Language: Japanese
Literacy: 100%
Income per capita: $41,000
Religions: Shinto or Buddhist 60%,
    indigenous 24%, nonreligious 14%,
    Roman Catholic 1%, Protestant 1%

Though still one of the wealthiest nations in the world, **Japan** has suffered persistent recession in recent years. PRAY that hard times would cause many Japanese to seek out the true riches Christ offers. Pray that this nation so important to the prosperity and stability of Asia will become a major influence for Christ in that part of the world as well.

Jordan

Population: 4,210,000

Capital: Amman

Language: Arabic

Literacy: 82%

Income per capita: $4,300

Religions: Muslim 94%, Orthodox 3%,
  Roman Catholic 2%

Having declared itself officially at peace with Israel in recent years, Jordan must still seek to maintain peace with the majority of Middle Eastern nations which share its Muslim/Arab heritage. With almost no evangelical believers, Jordan is nonetheless an important post of gospel outreach to other Arab nations. PRAY for the safety and success of Jordanians seeking to share their faith in Christ.

Kenya

Population: 28,180,000

Capital: Nairobi

Language: English, Swahili

Literacy: 69%

Income per capita: $1,200

Religions: non-Anglican Protestant 27%, Roman Catholic 22%,
  indigenous 19%, indigenous Christian 18%, Anglican 7%,
  Muslim 6%

Kenya, famed for its wildlife refuges, has suffered from high unemployment, inflation, and inter-tribal violence. Though Kenya's churches are often lukewarm in their faith, recent years have seen enthusiastic and successful outreach efforts by homegrown evangelistic and mission ministries. PRAY that Kenyans of all tribal groups will find a common ground in Christ.

North Korea

Population: 23,900,000

Capital: Pyongyang

Language: Korean

Literacy: 99%

Income per capita: $920

Religions: nonreligious 67%, indigenous 29%,
   Buddhist 2%, Christian 1%

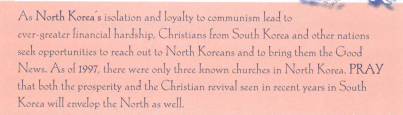

As North Korea's isolation and loyalty to communism lead to
ever-greater financial hardship, Christians from South Korea and other nations
seek opportunities to reach out to North Koreans and to bring them the Good
News. As of 1997, there were only three known churches in North Korea. PRAY
that both the prosperity and the Christian revival seen in recent years in South
Korea will envelop the North as well.

South Korea

Population: 45,480,000

Capital: Seoul

Language: Korean

Literacy: 96%

Income per capita: $8,500

Religions: Buddhist 33%, indigenous 24%,
   indigenous Christian 14%, Confucian 12%,
   Protestant 12%, Roman Catholic 4%

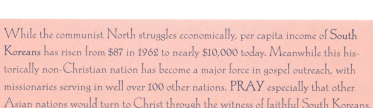

While the communist North struggles economically, per capita income of South
Koreans has risen from $87 in 1962 to nearly $10,000 today. Meanwhile this historically non-Christian nation has become a major force in gospel outreach, with
missionaries serving in well over 100 other nations. PRAY especially that other
Asian nations would turn to Christ through the witness of faithful South Koreans.

Lebanon

Population: 3,780,000

Capital: Beirut

Language: Arabic, French

Literacy: 80%

Income per capita: $4,400

Religions: Muslim 68%, Maronite Catholic 16%,
    Druze 7%, Orthodox 5%, Greek Catholic 3%

Though still recovering from the devastation of civil war,
and still surrounded by the instability of Middle Eastern
politics, **Lebanon** shows signs of once again becoming a major industrial and com-
mercial center. PRAY that the spiritual hunger created by the suffering of recent
years will turn more and more Lebanese to Christ. Pray that Lebanon will once
again become an outpost of gospel witness to the Arab world.

Lesotho

Population: 1,970,000

Capital: Maseru

Language: English, Sesotho

Literacy: 59%

Income per capita: $1,340

Religions: Roman Catholic 45%, Protestant 35%,
    indigenous Christian 13%, indigenous 6%

Slightly larger than Vermont, the mountainous nation of **Lesotho**
is completely surrounded by South Africa, and many of its people go there to find
work. While churches have a major influence in Lesotho's education system,
PRAY that this outreach would more and more include a strong gospel witness.
Pray for the continued success of youth ministries and of medical ministries to
remote mountain villages.

Lithuania

Population: 3,720,000

Capital: Vilnius

Language: Lithuanian

Literacy: 99%

Income per capita: $1,100

Religions: Roman Catholic 80%, nonreligious 13%, Orthodox 5%, Protestant 1%

The former Soviet republic of **Lithuania** is making slow but steady progress in its transition to democracy and capitalism. There is little spiritual life in the predominant Roman Catholic Church, and less than 1 percent would call themselves evangelical. PRAY that the few who have professed faith in Christ in recent years would remain faithful to him, and desire to bring others to him.

Luxembourg

Population: 410,000

Capital: Luxembourg

Language: Luxembourgish, French

Literacy: 100%

Income per capita: $22,000

Religions: Roman Catholic 95%, nonreligious 2%, Protestant 1%, Muslim 1%

Slightly smaller than Rhode Island, with only half as many people, **Luxembourg** nonetheless plays a key role in European politics and has a strong economy based on steel and banking. The country has very few evangelical churches. PRAY for more effective gospel outreach, to the people of Luxembourg and to the many from other nations who come there for employment or on corporate or governmental business.

Malaysia

Population: 19,960,000
Capital: Kuala Lumpur
Language: Malay, Chinese
Literacy: 78%
Income per capita: $4,000
Religions: Muslim 54%, indigenous 20%,
  Buddhist 7%, Hindu 6%, Protestant 5%,
  Roman Catholic 4%, nonreligious 3%

Divided geographically but united politically, **Malaysia** has grown wealthy from oil, timber, mining, and manufacturing. It recently completed the world's tallest building and is planning the world's longest as well. Muslim fundamentalists have brought much pressure against Christians, with home church meetings forbidden and permits for new church buildings denied. PRAY for a church equal to these challenges.

Mauritius

Population: 1,140,000
Capital: Port Louis
Language: English, French
Literacy: 83%
Income per capita: $8,600
Religions: Hindu 50%, Roman Catholic 25%, Muslim 12%,
  Protestant 7%, nonreligious 4%

The island nation of **Mauritius** prospers on sugar, tourism, and light manufacturing. Its economy grew rapidly in the past three years as it offered its people interest-free loans to invest in local stocks, while also becoming a tax haven for banks from other nations. The gospel has made some progress despite steady opposition. PRAY that the one true way to God would win many hearts in this wealthy nation of many religions.

Mexico

Population: 95,770,000
Capital: Mexico City
Language: Spanish
Literacy: 88%
Income per capita: $7,900
Religions: Roman Catholic 88%, Protestant 6%,
   nonreligious 4%

As many in northern **Mexico** find greater wealth due
to economic reforms and the North American Free Trade
Agreement, those in more remote areas are still in dire poverty—as reflected in recent Marxist guerrilla activity in the south.
Meanwhile, the gospel goes forth despite both anti-American and anti-
evangelical opposition. PRAY that the gospel will be heard at all levels of
Mexican society.

Moldova

Population: 4,460,000
Capital: Chisinau
Language: Moldovan, Russian
Literacy: 99%
Income per capita: $2,700
Religions: Orthodox 65%,
   nonreligious 27%, Catholic 3%,
   Jewish 2%, Protestant 2%

Moldova's abundant black soil gives it great potential as an agricultural exporter,
but development has been hampered by continuing political and ethnic strife.
Severely persecuted in communist days, evangelical Christians are few in number
and often lack adequate leadership and meeting places. PRAY that the Good
News of eternal salvation will be welcomed by a nation victimized by history and
indoctrinated by the communist version of truth.

Mongolia

Population: 2,500,000

Capital: Ulan Bator

Language: Mongolian

Literacy: 90%

Income per capita: $1,800

Religions: indigenous 50%, Buddhist 25%,
   nonreligious 20%, Muslim 4%

Since privatizing its economy in the early nineties, formerly
communist **Mongolia** has struggled to become self-sufficient. Meanwhile its vast
mineral wealth lies largely untapped due to lack of mining equipment and electrici-
ty. Evangelical churches are small but enthusiastic and fast-growing. PRAY for an
adequate presentation of the gospel in this Buddhist and animistic nation with little
knowledge of the one true God.

Mozambique

Population: 17,880,000

Capital: Maputo

Language: Portuguese

Literacy: 33%

Income per capita: $610

Religions: indigenous 38%, Roman Catholic 23%, Protestant 14%,
   Muslim 13%, indigenous Christian 5%, nonreligious 4%

Mozambique's independence from Portugal in 1975 was followed
by many years of oppressive communist rule. Now, as it allows greater economic
freedom, Mozambique allows greater religious freedom as well, and evangelical
churches have thrived. PRAY for missionaries and national church leaders who
can disciple new believers, train additional leaders, and take the gospel to the
nation's 200-plus language groups.

Myanmar (formerly Burma)

Population: 49,980,000
Capital: Yangon (Rangoon)
Language: Burmese
Literacy: 81%
Income per capita: $930
Religions: Buddhist 87%, Protestant 5%,
   Muslim 4%, indigenous 2%,
   Roman Catholic 1%, Hindu 1%

Myanmar has suffered in recent years from severe political oppression, which has led to economic problems as other nations have refused to do business with it. Meanwhile the church has prospered. Per capita, Myanmar sends out twice as many missionaries as the United States! PRAY that the church will remain strong. Pray for the encouragement of Bible translators who lost precious manuscripts to a fire in 1995.

Nepal

Population: 22,100,000
Capital: Katmandu
Language: Nepali
Literacy: 36%
Income per capita: $1,100
Religions: Hindu 90%, Buddhist 5%,
   Muslim 3%

Forty years ago there were no known Christians in the Hindu nation of **Nepal.** Today, despite ongoing persecution, there are more than 100,000, and recent evangelistic efforts have seen a good response. Thank God for this historic turnaround and PRAY that the hopeless religiosity of Hinduism will continue to give way to the truth of a real and living God who has entered human history to redeem his people.

Netherlands

Population: 15,530,000

Capital: The Hague

Language: Dutch

Literacy: 99%

Income per capita: $17,900

Religions: Roman Catholic 36%, nonreligious 30%, Protestant 28%, Muslim 3%, Hindu 1%

The **Netherlands** is a major power in the international exchange of goods and services—and in the international exchange of ideas as well. Though influential in Christian history, in recent years the Netherlands has become more well known for its advocacy of things such as legalized prostitution and physician-assisted euthanasia. PRAY for Dutch Christians seeking to turn their nation back to God.

Niger

Population: 9,110,000

Capital: Niamey

Language: French, Hausa

Literacy: 28%

Income per capita: $550

Religions: Muslim 90%, indigenous 9%

Niger has long been an impoverished nation, and the relentless approach of the Sahara Desert makes its situation even more desperate. There is greater hope for pushing back the spiritual desert of Islam. Witness to Muslims is permitted, and some are responding. PRAY that evangelical believers, though few in number, will see the great spiritual need all around them. Pray especially for more effective outreach to youth.

Nigeria

Population: 103,900,000
Capital: Abuja
Language: English, Hausa
Literacy: 51%
Income per capita: $1,300
Religions: Muslim 40%, non-Anglican Protestant 15%, Roman Catholic 12%, Anglican 10%, indigenous 10%, indigenous Christian 10%

Its vast oil wealth seems to have been a curse to **Nigeria**, leading to government instability and corruption while inflation rises and most people remain poor. Added to that are many ongoing tribal and religious conflicts. Three Christian schools were recently ordered to close because they wouldn't teach Islam. PRAY that Nigerian Christians will more effectively reach out to their Muslim neighbors.

Norway

Population: 4,350,000
Capital: Oslo
Language: Norwegian
Literacy: 100%
Income per capita: $22,200
Religions: Protestant 94%, nonreligious 4%

Second only to Saudi Arabia in oil production, **Norway** also thrives on fishing and timber. Its scenic coastline brings in tourist dollars and its high mountains provide the water and hydroelectric power for industry. There are many strong Christians in Norway's churches. PRAY that Norwegians will continue proclaiming Christ at home and through their many vibrant mission agencies.

Pakistan

Population: 129,280,000
Capital: Islamabad
Language: Urdu, English
Literacy: 35%
Income per capita: $1,900
Religions: Muslim 95%, Hindu 2%, Christian 2%

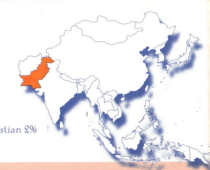

Pakistan faces constant pressure to conform its society to fundamentalist Islam. For Christians this means persecution and restriction of missionary activity. Several Christians in recent years have died mysteriously while in police custody. PRAY for the few and very courageous Muslim converts, who are often rejected by family and friends and are not always accepted by other Christians, most of whom are from a Hindu background.

Papua New Guinea

Population: 4,390,000
Capital: Port Moresby
Language: English, Melanesian pidgin
Literacy: 52%
Income per capita: $2,000
Religions: non-Anglican Protestant 59%,
    Roman Catholic 33%, Anglican 5%, indigenous 3%

Though nearly a quarter of its people claim faith in Christ, most of Papua New Guinea's 700 ethnic groups still have no Scripture in their own language. PRAY for the many Bible translators working in this rugged land, many of whom have dedicated their lives to reaching tribes in isolated places numbering no more than a few hundred souls. Pray that those receiving new Bibles will apply God's written Word to their lives.

Philippines

Population: 74,480,000
Capital: Manila
Language: Tagalog, English
Literacy: 94%
Income per capita: $2,300
Religions: Roman Catholic 65%,
    indigenous Christian 8%, Protestant 8%,
    other Catholic 8%, Muslim 8%

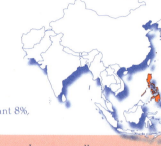

Though the **Philippines** continues to struggle economically, it
has been a major success story of gospel outreach. The number of foreign
missionaries currently in the Philippines is nearly matched by the number of
Filipino missionaries serving in other nations. PRAY for an adequate supply of
good leadership, and that the missionary vision will continue to grow. Pray for a
greater response among Muslims.

Portugal

Population: 9,870,000
Capital: Lisbon
Language: Portuguese
Literacy: 85%
Income per capita: $10,200
Religions: Roman Catholic 94%,
    nonreligious 4%, Protestant 1%

Years of dictatorship and socialism made **Portugal** the poorest country of Western
Europe. With greater political freedom in recent years, its prospects are improving.
Evangelical churches are growing steadily, yet only a third of them have pastors.
PRAY for leadership for these churches. Pray that Portugal will become a center for
producing Bibles and Christian literature for the world's nearly 200 million speak-
ers of Portuguese.

Around the World

Qatar

Population: 550,000

Capital: Doha

Language: Arabic, English

Literacy: 76%

Income per capita: $20,800

Religions: Muslim 91%, Roman Catholic 3%,
Protestant 3%, Hindu 2%

Qatar, a flat desert peninsula with almost no natural
vegetation, has grown rich on oil and has more recently
developed an industrial base. More independent than some Arab nations, it has
sought stronger ties with both Iran and Israel. The few Christians in Qatar are
almost all foreign guest workers. PRAY that Qataris who have become believers
while abroad will courageously share Christ when they return home.

Romania

Population: 21,660,000

Capital: Bucharest

Language: Romanian, Hungarian

Literacy: 98%

Income per capita: $2,800

Religions: Orthodox 67%, nonreligious 14%,
Protestant 11%, Roman Catholic 6%

Romania, which suffered greatly under communism, has not entirely abandoned
that system and still suffers much political uncertainty and economic hardship. As
their wages plummeted and inflation skyrocketed, many Romanians in 1993 lost
money in a nationwide pyramid scheme. PRAY that hardship, misfortune, and
uncertainty will turn many to Christ. Pray for committed Christians to disciple new
believers.

Russia

Population: 148,190,000
Capital: Moscow
Language: Russian
Literacy: 100%
Income per capita: $4,800
Religions: Orthodox 55%, nonreligious
   33%, Muslim 9%, Protestant 1%

Post-communist **Russia** continues to face economic hardship and political uncertainties. The resurgence of Russian nationalism has often led to laws favoring the Russian Orthodox church and restricting the rights of evangelicals. Nonetheless, the democratic era has seen the establishment of some 4,000 new evangelical churches and more than 100 Bible schools. PRAY especially for these schools as they train church leaders.

Rwanda

Population: 6,850,000
Capital: Kigali
Language: Kinyarwanda, French
Literacy: 61%
Income per capita: $950
Religions: Roman Catholic 46%, non-Anglican Protestant 22%,
   indigenous 17%, Muslim 8%, Anglican 6%

The long-term civil war between the Hutu and Tutsi ethnic groups of **Rwanda** and Burundi has continued in recent years, spilling over into Zaire, which is also devastated by civil strife. PRAY for the health and safety of all the innocent people caught up in this conflict, and for the relief workers seeking to help them. Pray that the Christianity most of these people profess will somehow be applied to this seemingly hopeless situation.

Saudi Arabia

Population: 19,410,000

Capital: Riyadh

Language: Arabic, English

Literacy: 65%

Income per capita: $9,500

Religions: Muslim 94%, Roman Catholic 3%,
   Protestant 1%

Saudi Arabia, long America's most dependable ally in
the Muslim/Arab world, has faced increasing instability in recent years as its
economy falters and Muslim extremists gain popularity. This has also meant
increased oppression of the few Christians who live there. PRAY that these faithful believers will continue to courageously bear witness to Christ.

Solomon Islands

Population: 410,000

Capital: Honiara

Language: English, Pidgin

Literacy: 30%

Income per capita: $2,600

Religions: Protestant 73%, Roman Catholic 19%,
   indigenous 6%

Most Solomon Islanders are subsistence farmers. Hardwoods are a major export,
but deforestation is a growing concern. America fought the Japanese on
Guadalcanal, the largest of the islands, during World War II, and many returned
as missionaries after the war. Most of the nation has been evangelized, and many
Islanders have gone as missionaries to other lands. PRAY for continued growth
and outreach.

South Africa

Population: 41,740,000
Capital: Pretoria
Language: English, Afrikaans
Literacy: 76%
Income per capita: $3,100
Religions: non-Anglican Protestant 39%,
    indigenous Christian 22%, indigenous 16%,
    Roman Catholic 10%, Anglican 7%, Hindu 2%

As **South Africa** deals with unemployment as high as 40 percent among blacks, it seeks the kind of stability that will convince foreign companies that left during the years of apartheid to return. PRAY that South Africa's many committed Christians, who played a vital role in ending apartheid, will continue to lead the nation toward lasting peace—and toward the Prince of Peace.

Spain

Population: 38,850,000
Capital: Madrid
Language: Spanish
Literacy: 97%
Income per capita: $13,100
Religions: Roman Catholic 78%,
    nonreligious 20%, Protestant 1%

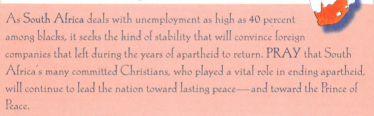

As it continues to break from its past of rigid state control, **Spain** is privatizing state-owned industries and welcoming a flood of foreign investment. As a predominantly Roman Catholic nation, it has not been quite so welcoming of evangelical missionaries. PRAY that both missionaries and Spanish evangelicals will find ways to reach nominal Catholics as well as the growing number of Spaniards who profess no religious faith.

Sri Lanka

Population: 18,550,000

Capital: Colombo

Language: Sinhala, Tamil

Literacy: 89%

Income per capita: $3,200

Religions: Buddhist 65%, Hindu 18%, Muslim 8%, Roman Catholic 7%, Protestant 1%

Sri Lanka, having survived years of civil strife, is reclaiming its place as the world's leading producer of tea and is developing a substantial clothing and textile industry. Many nominal Christians have converted to the more popular Hindu and Buddhist faiths——which has led committed Christians to a renewed concern for the lost. PRAY that Sri Lankan Christians, though a small minority, will speak out boldly for their Lord.

Switzerland

Population: 7,120,000

Capital: Bern

Language: German, French

Literacy: 99%

Income per capita: $22,100

Religions: Roman Catholic 47%, Protestant 42%, nonreligious 8%, Muslim 1%

Secure in its mountain fortress, Switzerland has been an economic powerhouse and mediating political force for generations. While the country's older Protestant churches decline rapidly, newer Bible-teaching churches are taking their places. PRAY that these new churches will become a strong influence for the gospel. Pray for the faithfulness of Swiss missionaries: Per capita, Switzerland sends slightly more missionaries than the U.S.

Syria

Population: 15,600,000

Capital: Damascus

Language: Arabic

Literacy: 64%

Income per capita: $5,000

Religions: Muslim 89%, Orthodox 6%,
   Roman Catholic 3%, Protestant 1%

Syria's economy has suffered in recent years due to its
military spending in its fight against Israel. The breakup of
the Soviet Union, its main trading partner, was another blow, but now Kuwait
and other oil-rich states—whom Syria helped in the Gulf War—are coming to
its aid. PRAY that Syria's Christians, a respected and influential minority, will
also be strong witnesses for Christ despite the official restrictions on such witness.

Thailand

Population: 58,850,000

Capital: Bangkok

Language: Thai

Literacy: 93%

Income per capita: $6,000

Religions: Buddhist 93%, Muslim 3%,
   indigenous 2%, Christian 1%

Thailand has remained relatively peaceful and prosperous amid an often turbulent
Southeast Asia. It is slowly transforming itself from an agricultural to an industrial
economy. Though many missionaries have gone to Thailand, it remains one of the
most unevangelized nations. The few converts are mostly from various minority
groups. PRAY for a spiritual breakthrough in this very resistant land.

Togo

Population: 4,570,000

Capital: Lomé

Language: Ewé, French

Literacy: 43%

Income per capita: $800

Religions: indigenous 36%, Roman Catholic 32%,
Muslim 20%, Protestant 9%, indigenous Christian 2%

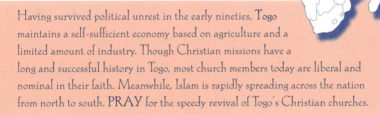

Having survived political unrest in the early nineties, Togo
maintains a self-sufficient economy based on agriculture and a
limited amount of industry. Though Christian missions have a
long and successful history in Togo, most church members today are liberal and
nominal in their faith. Meanwhile, Islam is rapidly spreading across the nation
from north to south. PRAY for the speedy revival of Togo's Christian churches.

Trinidad and Tobago

Population: 1,270,000

Capital: Port-of-Spain

Language: English

Literacy: 98%

Income per capita: $11,300

Religions: Roman Catholic 30%, Protestant 28%,
Hindu 24%, nonreligious 9%, Muslim 6%

The twin-island nation of Trinidad and Tobago enjoys a mea-
sure of prosperity based mainly on exports of sugar, oil, and
asphalt. However, unemployment runs at 20 percent, and there
is ongoing unrest between the Afro-Caribbean and East Indian racial groups.
Some 10 percent of the people claim to be evangelical Christians. PRAY for continued success in bringing Hindus to Christ, and that Muslims would also
respond.

Tunisia

Population: 9,020,000
Capital: Tunis
Language: Arabic, French
Literacy: 65%
Income per capita: $1,800
Religions: Muslim 99%

With the star and crescent on its flag, **Tunisia** is one of the world's most totally Muslim nations. Though tolerant of foreign religious minorities, it discourages conversion of Muslims. Less than 100 Tunisian nationals are known to be evangelical Christians. PRAY that the Tunisian government will win its ongoing battle with the most extreme Muslims. Pray for fruit from Arabic Christian television programs now available by satellite from Cyprus.

Ukraine

Population: 50,860,000
Capital: Kiev
Language: Ukrainian
Literacy: 99%
Income per capita: $3,700
Religions: Orthodox 55%,
   nonreligious 26%,
   Ukrainian Catholic 15%, Protestant 3%

Hard-pressed economically, the former Soviet republic of **Ukraine** continues to spend 10 percent of its national budget dealing with the results of the deadly Chernobyl nuclear disaster of 1986. Meanwhile, the government's need for cash has opened up its state-owned airwaves to Christian radio and television broadcasts. PRAY that many in Ukraine and nearby nations will see and hear, and respond.

United Kingdom

Population: 58,490,000
Capital: London
Language: English
Literacy: 99%
Income per capita: $18,000
Religions: Anglican 50%, nonreligious 26%,
   non-Anglican Protestant 10%,
   Roman Catholic 9%, Muslim 3%, Jewish 1%

Having survived for a thousand years in vari-
ous forms, the **United Kingdom** (England, Scotland, Wales, and
Northern Ireland) remains one of the world's most influential nations. Yet widespread abandonment of its traditional Christian faith and moral values is evidenced
by the fact that only one in four of its families has both a mother and father living at
home. PRAY for a new spiritual awakening.

United States

Population: 265,090,000
Capital: Washington, D.C.
Language: English
Literacy: 98%
Income per capita: $22,800
Religions: Protestant 56%, Roman Catholic 28%,
   nonreligious 7%, Jewish 3%, Orthodox 3%,
   Muslim 2%

The **United States of America** has enjoyed great prosperity in recent years. Spiritually, the signals are more mixed. While
new evangelical churches grow, most older denominations decline. One
spiritual barometer is the survey finding that Americans spend more on lotteries
than they give to churches. PRAY that America's wealth, and its unquenchable
desire for more wealth, will not blind it to its deep spiritual need.

Uzbekistan

Population: 23,420,000

Capital: Tashkent

Language: Uzbek, Russian

Literacy: 100%

Income per capita: $2,400

Religions: Muslim 68%,
    nonreligious 26%, Orthodox 4%

For many years, **Uzbekistan** was closed to the
gospel due to both communist control and the Muslim religion. Now, despite persecution, Christian churches are springing up and hundreds are responding to the gospel. **PRAY** that these new believers will turn their whole nation to Christ, and that they will become a powerhouse of evangelism throughout the Muslim world.

Vietnam

Population: 73,980,000

Capital: Hanoi

Language: Vietnamese

Literacy: 88%

Income per capita: $1,100

Religions: Buddhist 51%, nonreligious 30%,
    Roman Catholic 9%, indigenous 8%,
    Protestant 1%

Although **Vietnam** has increasingly sought diplomatic and economic ties with the United States, recent years have also seen continuing persecution of Christians—especially of the Hmong tribespeople, who were such faithful U.S. allies during the Vietnam War. **PRAY** that Hmong churches will continue their steady growth. Pray that the closer economic ties will bring opportunities for Western missions to bring the gospel to all of Vietnam.

Around the World

Yemen

Population: 13,480,000
Capital: Sanaa
Language: Arabic
Literacy: 38%
Income per capita: $2,000
Religions: Muslim 99%

Far less wealthy than its neighbors on the Arabian Peninsula, **Yemen** survives on limited oil exports and the agricultural produce of its western mountains. Virtually all Yemenis are Muslims, with the few who are Christians worshiping in secret. PRAY that Christians from other lands who are employed in Yemen will find creative ways to share their faith and to encourage Yemeni believers.

Yugoslavia (Serbia and Montenegro)

Population: 10,610,000
Capital: Belgrade
Language: Serbo-Croatian
Literacy: 91%
Income per capita: $1,000
Religions: Orthodox 67%, Muslim 17%,
  nonreligious 9%, Catholic 6%

Of the eight republics of the former Yugoslavia, only **Serbia** and **Montenegro** remain together under that name. Serbia's desire to unite all Serbs in former Yugoslavia has led to war in recent years. Even the very few evangelical Christians in this area find their churches torn apart by the bitterness and mistrust brought on by the war. PRAY for peace, among the various ethnic groups and among Christians.

Zaire

Population: 46,500,000
Capital: Kinshasa
Language: French, English
Literacy: 72%
Income per capita: $440
Religions: Roman Catholic 41%, Protestant 36%,
indigenous Christian 17%, indigenous 3%

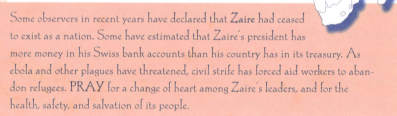

Some observers in recent years have declared that **Zaire** had ceased
to exist as a nation. Some have estimated that Zaire's president has
more money in his Swiss bank accounts than his country has in its treasury. As
ebola and other plagues have threatened, civil strife has forced aid workers to aban-
don refugees. PRAY for a change of heart among Zaire's leaders, and for the
health, safety, and salvation of its people.

Zimbabwe

Population: 11,270,000
Capital: Harare
Language: English, Ndebele
Literacy: 74%
Income per capita: $1,600
Religions: indigenous 33%, non-Anglican Protestant 27%,
indigenous Christian 15%, Roman Catholic 14%,
Anglican 6%

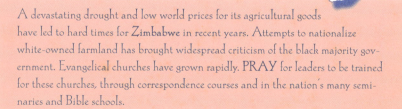

A devastating drought and low world prices for its agricultural goods
have led to hard times for **Zimbabwe** in recent years. Attempts to nationalize
white-owned farmland has brought widespread criticism of the black majority government. Evangelical churches have grown rapidly. PRAY for leaders to be trained
for these churches, through correspondence courses and in the nation's many seminaries and Bible schools.

Remember these other nations . . .

The worldwide family of nations is nearly two hundred strong. Space allows the inclusion of only about half of those nations in this volume. The following were not included, but deserve a place in our prayers.

Afghanistan
Albania
Algeria
Andorra
Angola
Antigua/Barbuda
Argentina
Azerbaijan
Bahamas
Bahrain
Belgium
Belize
Bhutan
Brunei Darussalam
Bulgaria
Burundi
Cambodia
Cameroon
Central African Republic
Chad
Chile
Congo
Cote d'Ivoire
Croatia
Cyprus
Denmark
Dominica
Ecuador
El Salvador
Estonia
Fiji
Finland
Gambia
Georgia
Grenada

Guinea-Bissau
Guyana
Honduras
Hungary
Iceland
Ireland
Jamaica
Kazakhstan
Kiribati
Kuwait
Kyrgyzstan
Laos
Latvia
Liberia
Libya
Liechtenstein
Macedonia
Madagascar
Malawi
Maldives
Mali
Malta
Marshall Islands
Mauritania
Micronesia
Monaco
Morocco
Namibia
Nauru
New Zealand
Nicaragua
Oman
Palau
Panama
Paraguay

Peru
Poland
San Marino
São Tomé/Príncipe
Senegal
Seychelles
Sierra Leone
Singapore
Slovakia
Slovenia
Somalia
St. Kitts/Nevis
St. Lucia
St. Vincent/Grenadines
Sudan
Suriname
Swaziland
Sweden
Tajikistan
Tanzania
Tonga
Turkey
Turkmenistan
Tuvalu
Uganda
United Arab Emirates
Uruguay
Vanuatu
Vatican City State
Venezuela
Western Samoa
Zambia

SOURCES

Christianity Today magazine.

The Church Around the World newsletter.

Lloyd Cory, *Quote Unquote* (Wheaton, Ill.: Scripture Press, 1977).

The 1997 Information Please Almanac (Boston: Houghton Mifflin, 1996).

Patrick Johnstone, *Operation World* (Grand Rapids, Mich.: Zondervan, 1993).

The New Dictionary of Thoughts (New York: Doubleday, 1977).

The Times Guide to the Nations of the World (London: HarperCollins, 1994).

U.S. News and World Report magazine.

Albert M. Wells, Jr., comp., *Inspiring Quotations* (Nashville: Thomas Nelson, 1988).

The World Almanac and Book of Facts, 1997 (Mahwah, N.J.: K-III Reference Corp., 1996).